WHIPLASH

THE FACTS
AUTO INSURANCE
COMPANIES
Don't Want You to Know
ABOUT REAR-END COLLISIONS

(don't settle your rear-end collision case without reading this first!)

D.L. BAKER

Produced by:
Specialty Products, LLC
P. O. Box 851
Lawrence, KS 66044

Contributing Author: Douglas Baker

Cover: Artwork is credited to Arthur Croft, Ph.D., D.C., M.Sc., M.P.H., F.A.C.O.
Spine Research Institute of San Diego, Inc.
Used by permission.

ISBN: 978-0-578-71123-2 (paperback)

Printed in the United States of America

June 2020

TABLE OF CONTENTS

PREFACE

This book contains information from thousands of medical journal articles on the significance of whiplash injuries, dozens of scientific studies, data from tens of thousands of rear-end automobile collisions, a compilation of research done by The Insurance Research Council, and notes, interviews and commentaries by some of the foremost personal injury attorneys, both plaintiff and defense, in the United States. *It is specifically not intended as legal advice, and therefore should not be considered as such.*

> *"Whiplash injuries are particularly complex because multiple body parts are injured simultaneously. The task of diagnosis and treatment is made more difficult, as the symptoms of cervical, TMJ and closed head injuries are similar."* [46]

If you, the reader, are the injured victim of a rear-end collision, you must be aware of how and why an injury can occur in what is generally described as a "fender bender". Armed with this knowledge, and an understanding a permanent injury is possible, you will then know which course of action to take. Should you: 1) attempt to negotiate a settlement without legal counsel; or, 2) hire an attorney. Hiring a competent lawyer is critically important to your future well-being. See page 73: "Selecting the Right Lawyer for Your Case". Negotiating your own whiplash case can be complicated and is not for the faint of heart. See page 77: "Should I Attempt to Settle the Case Myself".

The purpose of this book is to provide the auto-injured person with foundational knowledge about whiplash injuries, the mechanisms of injury—the "how" and "why" the injured person was hurt in a seemingly insignificant car wreck. The information will allow you to document for others, your family, friends and co-workers, there are real reasons for your injury, pain, and symptoms. It is a book about TRUTH. The purpose of this book is to give the person "on the street" enough information to understand the severity of the injury and different treatment methods that are effective; and, then, knowing the future possibility and/or probability the symptoms of the injury may be permanent, to select the best path of action. Is it better to hire an attorney or attempt a settlement on your own? If the decision is made to hire legal counsel, how to find an attorney knowledgeable about the intricacies of whiplash injuries.

The information contained in this book is accepted by knowledgeable professionals in medical and legal circles as being accurate. This information is readily available to those in the insurance industry. Many of the tests from which the conclusions herein were drawn were funded by the auto insurance industry. Why, then, do most auto insurance claims adjusters minimize occupant injuries and "overlook" obvious pertinent facts when negotiating an auto injury claim with an uninformed victim? [Answer: Money]

There are approximately three million rear-end collision cases annually in the United States. The actual number is likely higher because of the proliferation of cell phones and the number of drivers who text and drive. Often, there is a delay in onset of symptoms that are not reported. Automobile liability insurance for negligence is required in every state.

Each auto rear-end collision will involve an insurance company claims adjuster, whose job is to settle the claim with the injured victim as expeditiously, and as *economically*, as possible. Approximately 9,000 times a day, claims adjusters are reviewing the facts of a rear-end collision case through the eyes of training received from an insurance company. How many times in your life will you review the facts of a rear-end collision case in which you were injured? What kind of training have you had in evaluating the effects of the rear-end collision? How will you be able to negotiate a fair settlement with the insurance company? The negotiating edge goes to the trained and experienced. Consider for a moment the financial benefit to auto insurance companies if claims adjusters settle cases for One Thousand Dollars [$1,000.00] less than their real value. That amounts to an annual savings to the auto insurance industry of Three Billion Dollars [$3,000,000,000]. What if the settlement value, due to your inexperience and lack of information, was Five Thousand Dollars [$5,000.00] less than the real value of your case? The savings to the auto insurance industry would exceed Fifteen Billion Dollars [$15,000,000,000] annually. Settling whiplash personal injury cases for less than full value is BIG BUSINESS for auto insurance companies.

What is the fair value of your personal injury case? It is totally dependent upon how well you and/or your attorney are educated about rear-end collision cases and the resultant injuries. Reading this book will give you insights into how injury occurs, options for treatment, long term consequences and how to retain legal counsel. The principles, data and facts contained in this book are appropriate, to some extent, to all automobile collisions. However, the information contained herein is specific to rear-end collision incidents, especially those referred to by the auto insurance companies as M.I.S.T. cases: Minor Impact, Soft Tissue. The reference to Minor Impact means little property damage [which may not directly correspond to the force of impact or injuries received]. Soft Tissue refers to injuries to muscles, ligaments, nerves and connecting tissue. On page 5 is a list of the Eleven Myths insurance adjusters use to negotiate a settlement.

Each Myth is described in detail. Use the checklist at the end of the chapter to determine the probability of injury and the degree of seriousness for any resulting injury from your "incident". Please note the word 'accident' is deliberately omitted throughout this book, unless referenced in a quoted medical journal article. An example of an accident is a meteorite falling from the sky and landing on your vehicle. An accident is unavoidable. It is an "incident" when another driver negligently runs his/her vehicle into yours. It was avoidable. The other driver was likely not paying attention. It was not an accident: it was an "incident" for which the insurance company of the negligent driver is responsible to pay for damages, including personal injury to the occupants of the struck vehicle.

The author of this book highly recommends the following three things:

- Read this book in its entirety before negotiating with the auto insurance claims adjuster.
- Don't consider a settlement until the symptoms from your injuries are static and stable—usually 6 to 12 months following the incident; and,
- Use the guidelines in this book to interview and retain a competent and knowledgeable attorney.

For you or your attorney to effectively negotiate with the auto insurance claims adjuster it becomes necessary to know the TRUTH for each of the following Eleven Myths, especially those applicable to your incident. May your settlement be fair and equitable; your future driving safe and incident free; and, and may your injuries not be permanent.

Eleven Myths
Insurance Companies Want You to Believe About Whiplash Injuries

Myth No. 1: *Minor vehicle damage means inconsequential injury to the occupant.*

Myth No. 2: *The injury is a simple strain or sprain, and like a sprained ankle, will heal in 6—12 weeks.*

Myth No. 3: *The victim did not complain of pain at the scene of the wreck (or to the investigating officer) so if there was an injury, it must not be serious.*

Myth No. 4: *Men and women are equally at risk to suffer whiplash injury in a rear impact collision.*

Myth No. 5: *The victim's soft tissue injuries have continued to improve for 12 months, post rear-end collision. In another few months, he/she will be fully recovered.*

Myth No. 6: *Permanent injuries from a whiplash injury are rare.*

Myth No. 7: *When seat belt restrained and with a properly positioned head restraint or a high seat back, it is impossible for a whiplash injury to occur.*

Myth No. 8: *A whiplash injury does not affect a person's low back.*

Myth No. 9: *The victim is trying to get a big settlement for a minor injury. Once compensated, the symptoms and pain will go away.*

Myth No. 10: *Closed head injuries, or 'mild' traumatic brain injuries, do not occur in minor vehicle damage rear-end collisions.*

Myth No. 11: *TMJ (Temporomandibular Joint) injuries do not occur in minor vehicle damage rear-end collisions.*

INTRODUCTION

Auto insurance companies view rear-end collision cases from a much higher perch than the average citizen. Each year these insurance companies, often through The Insurance Research Council,* some of whose members are listed below, review hundreds of thousands, if not millions, of automobile collisions each year to determine incident trends such as average settlement value, severity of injuries, attorney involvement, chiropractic care, the incidence of fraud, the correlation between property damage and occupant injury, and a myriad of other issues, all in an effort to calculate cash reserves against future losses, which ultimately affects the insurance companies' bottom line. By manipulating how the reviewed data is presented to the public, the auto insurance industry can, and does, influence the public's perception of M.I.S.T. type cases. This was especially evident in the mid-1990s when a newspaper in a large metropolitan

---

* 2019 Auto Insurance Company Members of The Insurance Research Council include: Allstate Insurance Company, American Family Insurance, AMICA Mutual Insurance Company, Erie Insurance, Hanover Insurance Group, Liberty Mutual Group, National Association of Mutual Insurance Companies, American Property Casualty Insurance Association, Sentry Insurance, State Farm Insurance Companies and United Services Automobile Association.

area ran a full-page ad in the Sunday paper featuring a picture of an older car sitting at a Stop sign. The prominently displayed bumper sticker said: "Go ahead and hit me, I need the money". The auto insurance company was attempting to persuade the public that: 1) Rear-end collisions with minor property damage don't cause personal injury; and, 2) People who make claims for injury from these "fender benders" are just trying to scam the auto insurance companies. Sadly, many in the U.S. believe the statements to be true when the overwhelming evidence is the opposite. Medical and peer-reviewed studies show 95% of people claiming an injury in a rear-end collision are real people with real injuries.

The above described ad is just one example of how the auto insurance industry has perpetuated an even greater fraud on the public at large. Sure, there are documented cases of greedy and unscrupulous doctors, lawyers and their clients attempting to defraud the auto insurance industry through faked or exaggerated claims. The TRUTH is less than Five Percent (5%) of all personal injury claims submitted are fraudulent. Out of every one hundred (100) injury claims made, ninety-five [95] are made by real people with a very real injury, who just want to recover their health and be restored to their pre-incident condition. The auto insurance industry would have you believe the Eleven Myths on page 5 are true.

What is a Myth? *A Myth is defined as: "a collective opinion, belief or ideal that is based on false premises or is the product of fallacious meaning". A Myth is a half-truth, something that may be feasible, or possible, or may even seem probable, but after close examination, is found to be erroneous and untrue.* If intentionally presented as such, it is a lie. This presentation is about TRUTH. The bright light of medical, engineering, and legal scrutiny will shine on these Eleven [11] Myths to reveal the TRUTH.

MYTH NO. 1

Minor vehicle damage means minor or inconsequential occupant injury.

This statement can be true some of the time. However, as is shown below, it is not always the case regardless of what an auto insurance claims adjuster may say. In those incidents involving serious injury, there may be no correlation between property damage and the severity of injury.

> *"A substantial number of injuries are reported in crashes of little or no property damage. Property damage is an unreliable predictor of injury or outcome in low velocity crashes."* [1]

There is little correlation between the speed of the colliding vehicle and injury to the occupant of the struck vehicle.

> *"A 2005 study of 1,274 rear impacts in Germany found 40% - 50% of neck injuries occurred in rear impacts of 6 MPH or less."* [2]

Many people think no injury occurs to the occupant of a struck vehicle unless the striking vehicle was going fast and/or there is a lot of property damage to the struck vehicle. That is simply not true.

> "The majority of neck injuries that are reported in the medical literature in rear-end crashes, with symptoms lasting beyond one month, occurred in collisions where the speed of the bullet vehicle was 9.3—12.4 MPH." [7]

Note the following quote published in the Society of Automotive Engineers.

> "A common misconception formulated is that the amount of vehicle crash damage due to a collision offers a direct correlation to the degree of occupant injury." [3]

Another peer reviewed medical journal article appearing in the publication "Neurology", had this to say about occupant injury and vehicle damage.

> "The amount of damage to the automobile and the speed of the cars involved in the collision bear little relationship to the injury sustained by the cervical spine." [4]

If you have been injured in a rear-end collision you need to understand how the injury occurred. This will involve a short "crash course" in physics. There are two laws of physics applicable in every rear-end collision. The first is "The Law of Conservation of Linear Momentum", which is not nearly as daunting as it sounds. Simply stated, in a collision, at the point of impact, the energy is not lost but transferred along a linear plane. An excellent example of this is the game of billiards, or pool. When the cue ball hits the object ball, the energy is transferred to the object ball, and the object ball is knocked forward. The amount of force and energy with which the cue ball strikes the object ball determines how fast and how far the object ball will be propelled. This phenomenon is "Acceleration". This same principle is applied when one vehicle collides with another. There are several factors which determine the Acceleration of the struck vehicle. This is particularly important because *the acceleration of the vehicle has a direct correlation to occupant injury.*

DECREASING ACCELERATION of the struck vehicle lessens the likelihood of occupant injury. The following will decrease the Forward Acceleration of the struck vehicle.

- A smaller striking vehicle.
- A larger struck vehicle.
- The road conditions are dry.
- The struck vehicle is stationary at the moment of impact.
- The brakes are applied on the struck vehicle at the moment of impact; and,
- The struck vehicle has a manual transmission in low gear at the moment of impact.

INCREASING ACCELERATION of the struck vehicle increases the likelihood of occupant injury. The following will increase the Forward Acceleration of the struck vehicle.

- A larger striking vehicle.
- A smaller struck vehicle.
- The road conditions are wet or icy.
- The struck vehicle is moving at the moment of impact.
- The brakes are not applied on the struck vehicle at the moment of impact; and,
- The struck vehicle has an automatic transmission.

Consider this statement taken from the article "Acceleration Extension Injuries of the Cervical Spine" published in the scientific journal *The Spine.*

"Acceleration depends on the force applied and the inertia of the vehicle that has been struck. The force is dependent upon the weight and speed of the striking vehicle, so that a streetcar traveling at 3 MPH

can apply as much force and initiate the same degree of acceleration as a compact car traveling at 40 MPH. The inertia of the car that has been struck will depend not only on its weight but also on factors that will allow it to roll easily; for example, slippery road conditions, whether the brakes were on, automatic or standard transmission. A car that is moving slowly will accelerate more rapidly than one that is stationary." [5]

The critical question is: ***"What was the acceleration of the struck vehicle?"***

The second law of physics is "Magnification of Acceleration". Simply stated, this principle says the amount of force applied to the rear of the struck vehicle will be magnified and the acceleration of the occupant's head will be increased two to five times. Remember the game played as kids called "crack the whip". If you were on the inside part of the human chain, you did not move very fast. But, if you were at the opposite end of the lengthening arc, the speed at which the arc turned soon proved to be moving faster than you could run. The applied Law of Magnification of Acceleration may have been great fun in the kids' game of "crack the whip". It can have serious consequences for the occupants of the struck vehicle in a rear-end collision.

One of the first published scientific studies on the law of "Magnification of Acceleration" documented that in a controlled automobile rear-end collision, where the bullet vehicle was traveling 8.2 MPH, the stopped struck vehicle received 2 gravitational units of force [G-force]. The shoulder of the occupant received 4 gravitational units of force; and, the head of the occupant received 5 gravitational units of force. At higher speeds of 20 MPH, the head and neck may be subjected to five times the G-force applied to the rear of the struck vehicle. The graph on the following page shows the acceleration of the vehicle, the shoulder, and the head in a time lapsed sequence.

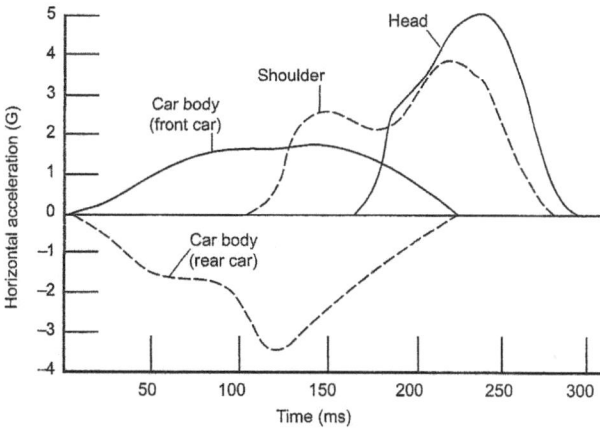

Within .3 seconds of impact, the head reaches an acceleration of 2 to 2.5 times the maximum vehicle acceleration, which is faster than the body can react to protect itself.

The acceleration noted in the graph happens literally within the blink of an eye, or about three tenths (3/10ths) of one second. This is a critical factor in determining injury. Within 3/10ths of a second of impact, the head reaches acceleration 2.5 times the maximum vehicle acceleration, **which is faster than the body can react to protect itself.**

"It has been shown that when a 3,500-pound car traveling at 10 MPH strikes the rear end of another car, it may transmit to this car a force of 25 tons. The person's body (in the car that is struck) continues to move forward while the head, being hinged at the neck, snaps backward. The average head weighs about 8 pounds, and the cervical vertebrae are very delicate; the force that is pushing the head backward is even greater than believed, since the base of the neck acts as a fulcrum and the leverage is applied near the top of the head. Therefore, the head snaps back with the equivalent of several tons of force—without any support, since 'the muscle control of the neck is caught off guard'. The end result, with the neck in acute hyperextension, is a momentary posterior subluxation of the various joints with fleeting narrowing of the foramina, so that the nerve root is caught in a pincher between the superior and inferior facets." [6]

What does that mean in plain English? It means the nerve branches that come out from the spinal cord [in the neck region] and travel down the arm to the hand and fingers, get pinched by the vertebrae of the neck when it is extended or flexed *beyond its normal range of motion*. This causes bruising and bleeding to the nerve root, at a minimum. At worst, it can cause a tearing, or shearing, of the nerve root. In either instance, scarring of the nerve root occurs and this results in a permanent condition known as "perineural fibrosis" [See description of condition on page 24].

The diagram on the following two pages shows the movement of an occupant in a vehicle struck by another. Please note the time sequence graph that appears in the upper left-hand corner of each illustration is the same as that appearing on the prior page. *Injury can occur before the body has the chance to react and protect itself.*

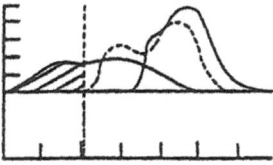

Fig. 1

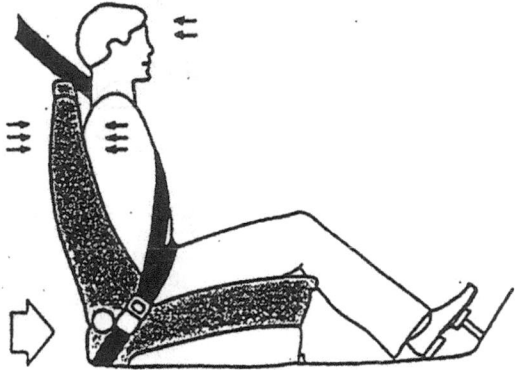

Fig. 2

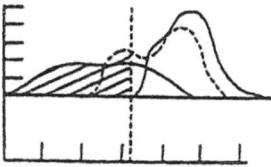

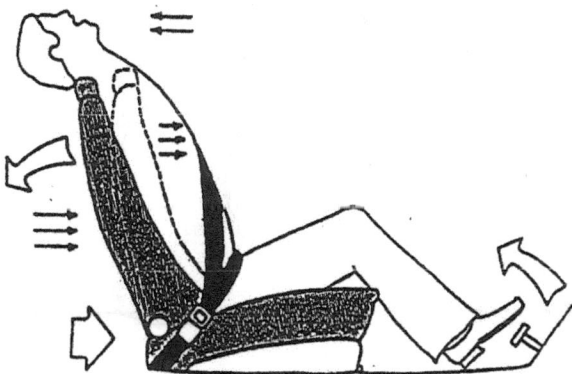

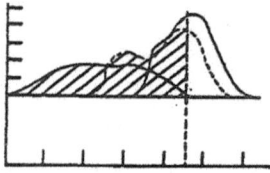

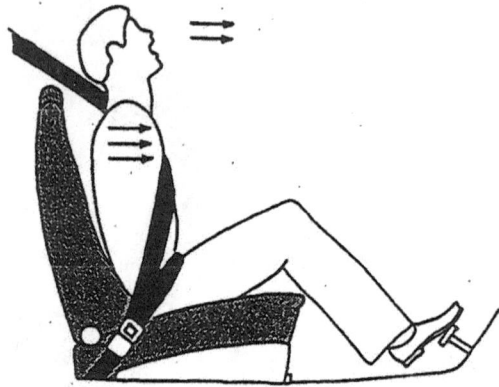

Fig. 3

Fig. 4

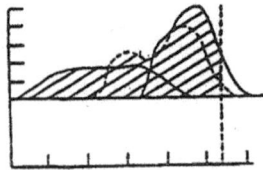

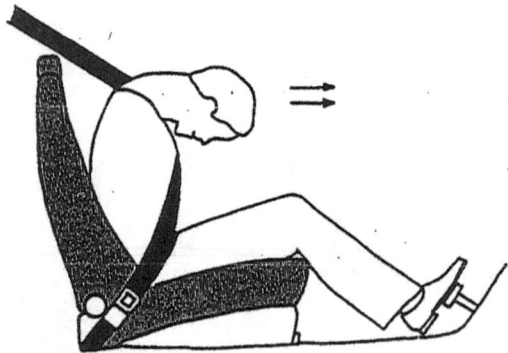

COMMON SYMPTOMS OF WHIPLASH

Neckache

Neck "stiffness" with limited movement

Memory Impairment

Shoulder Pain

Tinnitus [Ringing in the Ears]

Visual Disturbances

Auditory Disturbances

Anxiety & Irritability

Fatigue

Headache

Dizziness

Sleeplessness

Tenderness

Weakness

Spasms

TMJ

Another way to think about the forces involved in what appears to be a minor impact is to note the scientific studies that show a 10 MPH rear-end collision generates forces equivalent to catching a 200-pound sack of cement tossed from a first story window. The forces in a 15 MPH rear impact are equivalent to falling from the top of a two-story building. There can be significant forces involved in these rear-end collision M.I.S.T. cases, often resulting in personal injury, with little or no property damage. How serious is the injury? Read the discussion of the next Myth to find out.

IN SUMMARY

MYTH NO. 1: *Minor vehicle damage means minor or inconsequential occupant injury.*

The two key points to remember regarding this myth are: 1) The Acceleration of the vehicle causes the injury. The weight, size and speed of the impacting vehicle affect Acceleration, as does the weight, size, and transmission of the struck vehicle. The condition of the road surface and whether the struck vehicle was moving are also factors determining the Acceleration of the struck vehicle. 2) Acceleration occurs in the blink of an eye (300 milliseconds). Injury occurs before the body can protect itself.

CHECKLIST—MYTH NO. 1

1. Was the striking vehicle larger or smaller than the struck vehicle?

2. What was the condition of the road—dry, or wet and/or icy?

3. Was the struck vehicle stationary or moving at the time of impact?

4. Does the struck vehicle have manual or automatic transmission?

5. Were the brakes being applied on the struck vehicle at the moment of impact?

MYTH NO. 2

The injury is a simple strain or sprain, and like a sprained ankle, will heal in 6-12 weeks.

A definition of strain and sprain is helpful in understanding the medical journal quotes which follow. If the muscle, tendon, or ligament is torn or ruptured, the injury is referred to as a sprain. If the muscle, tendon, or ligament stretches without rupture, the injury is referred to as a strain. Soft tissue tears—sprain. Soft tissue stretches but doesn't tear—strain. A strain or sprain may occur because the soft tissue exceeded its normal range of motion; or, it may occur because of the speed of the motion.

It is important to understand what is considered a normal range of motion, and the terms used in medical and scientific journals. *Extension* is the motion of the head and neck in a backwards motion. *Flexion* is the motion of the head and neck in a forward motion. *Hyper* means any motion beyond normal limits. Hyper-extension is the motion of the head and neck in a backwards motion beyond normal limits of movement. Hyper-flexion is the motion of the head and neck in a forward motion beyond normal limits of movement. The normal range of motion for a combined full flexion and extension is 120 degrees. In a rear-end collision, the head may hyperextend to 140 degrees. The potential for injury is high.

> *"The cervical spine consists of seven vertebrae. While damage to these bony structures does occur, and is serious, most all M.I.S.T. injuries involve either a "sprain" or "strain" to the ligaments and muscles of the neck and are therefore considered soft tissue injuries."* [8]

What is 'soft tissue'? It is anything that is not a bone. It is the muscles, connecting tissues, ligaments, tendons, and nerves. Soft tissues have 'stretch', similar to elastic, but when forced beyond their normal range of motion in 'the blink of an eye', these soft tissues can rupture and tear.

> *"Viscoelastic properties are displayed by all soft tissues; the rate of stretch is an important factor. When the rate is high, as is the case in moderate or high-level G-force, the ability of soft issues to resist injury is overcome. Stretching it slowly allows it to deform into a long string. Rapid stretch causes it to fracture into two short pieces."* [9]

What does this mean? As a kid did you ever play with Silly Putty? If you rolled it out in a piece shaped like a pencil, and then gently pulled at each end, the Silly Putty would stretch even longer. But, if you quickly jerked on each end, the Silly Putty would break in two. The same principle applies to a rear-end collision. Remember, the body is not able to protect itself because the extension and flexion occurs 'in the blink of an eye'. Even if the neck does not exceed the normal range of motion, an injury may occur because of the speed of the motion. In other words, the muscles, tendons, ligaments, and nerves may be ruptured by the speed of the movement.

One of the most frustrating aspects of whiplash injuries is the public's perception of the injuries, including the victim and treating health care professionals at the emergency room. The auto insurance industry's campaign to convince the public no one is injured in M.I.S.T. type collisions has been largely successful. Imagine you are the front seat female passenger in a smaller vehicle stopped at a traffic light. Your head is turned to the right as you watch a group of young people walking home from school in the snow. You are completely unaware of the impending collision by a large pickup truck travelling 15 MPH, its high school aged driver texting on a cell phone until the moment of impact. You have immediate pain in your neck, a screaming headache and you can hardly stand up due to dizziness. A police officer arrives at the scene in minutes. Noticing your disorientation, blurred vision, and your complaints of headache [and now nausea], he calls an ambulance. You are put on a transport board with a cervical collar and taken to the nearest hospital.

At the emergency room you are examined with the 3 Bs in mind: 1) Is the patient Breathing? 2) Is the patient Bleeding? 3) Are Bones Broken? You are breathing; you are not bleeding; and, no bones appear to be broken. To be certain, the doctor on call orders an X-ray, which may or may not show any abnormalities. Since you are not suffering from a life-threatening condition, you are not a candidate for further care at the hospital ER. You are sent home with a prescription for pain medication, an instruction sheet for the care of strain/sprain injuries and advised the situation will resolve in 6—12 weeks, just like a sprained ankle.

Three months later your headache is a daily occurrence, especially following physical activity. Your neck still causes pain and your range of motion is limited. You are always tired, a feeling you attribute to the fact your sleep is constantly being disrupted by the pain in your neck. Your family, friends and co-workers notice you aren't carrying your share of the load, and whispers about malingering start to crop up. You are told to "buck up, it was only a little fender bender". The auto insurance claims adjuster for the driver of the truck who hit you stops by a week after the wreck with photos of the two vehicles. There was minimal damage to the vehicle in which you were an occupant and no visible damage to the pickup truck. He offers to write you a check for $500 for the inconvenience—"just sign this Release". No mention of injuries, how long it may take for the headaches and stiff neck to go away, or even if they will. Your family and friends think you should take the money. You are beginning to wonder if it's all in your head, that maybe you weren't really hurt. After all, the hospital personnel at the emergency room told you, in essence, it was no big deal. They said you would heal in a couple months. They are doctors and nurses: we should believe them, right? Unfortunately, when it comes to whiplash injuries, this is not always true. You are confused and unsure how to proceed. You know something is not right, but having never been in this situation, you can't put your finger on it. You get online and find this publication advising you not to settle with an auto insurance company for a whiplash type injury until you know more. You want to know how seriously you are injured, and when you are going to be normal again. When you read how six factors determine the severity of injury, you know you're not going to settle until you know the truth, and can be certain that, at a minimum, your future medical bills will be paid.

A basic premise of our American system of law is the injured party be returned to his/her pre-accident condition by the party at fault, by physical and/or mental restoration, or compensation. In other words, the victim is to be "made whole".

SEVERITY OF INJURY IS DEPENDENT ON SIX FACTORS

1. **FORCE OF IMPACT:** In our discussion of the first Myth [*Minor vehicle damage means minor or inconsequential occupant injury.*], the importance of the struck vehicle's acceleration was discussed. Please review the previous discussion for the importance of the elements of impact.

2. **OCCUPANT AWARENESS OF IMPENDING COLLISION:** The medical literature and scientific studies have repeatedly shown if the passenger is aware of and anticipates a collision, and makes his/her neck muscles tense, he/she can tolerate a more severe impact. That is the reason some volunteers in insurance company studies are not seriously injured: they know the collision is about to occur and they have

braced for the impact. This is also the reason why the driver of a vehicle about to be hit may not be injured if he/she saw the striking vehicle in time to brace for the impact. In the before described scenario the woman passenger with no notice of the impending collision, suffered a serious injury because she was unable to brace for the crash. Consider the following quotes from well-respected medical and scientific publications.

> *"Unaware occupants are fifteen times higher risk of having symptoms at six months [following a collision] as compared to aware occupants in rear-end crashes."* [47]

> *"Injury results because the neck is unable to adequately compensate for the rapidity of head and neck torso movement resulting from the acceleration forces generated at the time of impact. This is particularly true when the impact is unexpected, and the victim is unable to brace for it."* [10]

> *"In a whiplash injury, the acceleration-deceleration movements of the neck are typically completed within 250 milliseconds. The brevity of this period precludes any voluntary or reflex muscle response that might arrest, limit, or control the movements of a cervical motion segment. Without muscle control, the normal accurate movement of a cervical motion segment must be disturbed, and the forces to which individual segments are subjected can be resisted only by passive ligamentous elements or bony contact. This sets the scene for a variety of possible injuries."* [11]

Again, what does this mean in plain English? If you are *unaware* the vehicle in which you are an occupant is about to be hit by another vehicle, whether it's a rear impact or a side impact, you are at a much higher risk to receive an injury, especially to the 'soft tissue' in the neck region.

> *"In addition to the stretching and tearing of soft tissue [ligaments and muscles] beyond their normal limits, the spinal nerve may be*

caught in a pincer action, which leads to bruising, bleeding and scarring of the nerve sheath." (12)

The scarring that occurs during the healing process can cause additional future medical issues. As the torn tissue heals, the scar formation attaches to adjacent soft tissues, which upon movement will cause a tugging and pulling on the nerve, causing pain and discomfort. This condition is called perineural fibrosis. It is a **permanent condition!**

3. **POSITION OF OCCUPANT'S HEAD AT MOMENT OF IMPACT:** Here is an exercise you can do right now as you are reading this to demonstrate how the position of the occupant's head at the moment of impact can have a significant bearing on the severity of the injury. While sitting in a chair, with your back against the seat back, extend your head backwards as far as it will go. Note the furthest point on the ceiling you can see. Return to the front and rotate your head, to the right or left, 45 degrees. 90 degrees would be looking directly past your shoulder; 45 degrees is halfway from looking straight ahead to looking past your shoulder. Now, extend your head backwards as far as it will go, again noting the furthest point on the ceiling you can see. You are not able to extend the neck nearly as far when your head is rotated.

   "If the neck is rotated 45 degrees at the time of impact, the amount of cervical extension is reduced 50%." (13)

Why—because now there is bone hitting bone. Note the following quotes taken from medical journal articles regarding the potential for serious injury when the head is rotated at the moment of impact.

   "The possibility of sustaining a neck injury with long term consequences (more than three months) showed a significant correlation to the occupant having his head turned to the side at the time of impact." (48)

"When hyperextension-hyperflexion occurs with head rotation present, the pattern of tissue injury is different, and the extent of damage produced is always more severe. Rotation increases stress in certain soft tissue structures, which then reach their limit of motion at an earlier point, thus resulting in more severe injury with less application of force." [14]

"When the direction of force is from the side, or when a frontal or rear force occurs while the head is turned to one side, the spine is less flexible and the force is expanded upon the articulations where the small bone elements may be fractured." [15]

"Injuries are greater when nonsymmetrical loads are applied to the spine. This occurs when the spine sustains a rotary injury. The injuries are increased because the facet joints lock-out spinal motion, making the neck rigid, less resilient, and more susceptible to injury. When the head is rotated 45 degrees to one side, the amount of extension that side of the spine is capable of is decreased by 50%. This results in increased compressive loads on the facet joints, articular pillars on the ipsilateral side, and increased tensor loads at the facet joint on the contralateral side. The intervertebral foramen is smaller on the side of rotation and lateral flexion, and the neurovascular bundles are more vulnerable to compressive injuries." [16]

Again, what does this mean in plain English? When you look at the seven vertebrae of the neck you will observe bony "wings" on both sides of the vertebrae. When the head is rotated to one side at the moment of impact, these bony wings are compressed against each other. This can cause the bone elements to fracture and/or pinch the nerve root, which then leads to bruising, bleeding, and scarring of the nerve sheath. As previously noted, this is a **permanent condition** known as perineural fibrosis.

"If the head is in slight rotation, a rear-end impact will force the head into further rotation before extension occurs. This has

important consequences because cervical rotation pre-stresses various cervical structures, including capsules of the zygapophysial joints, inter-vertebral discs, and the alar ligament complex, making them more susceptible to injury." [17]

Research has shown a rupture of the capsule of a zygapophysial joint will result in chronic pain, which will then be a lifelong companion of the injured victim. Because the capsule is located deep within the structure of the neck, the injury is only discoverable by autopsy, a diagnostic procedure not favored by the auto injured victim.

4. **GENDER AND PHYSICAL BUILD OF OCCUPANT:** The gender and physical build of the vehicle occupant is a key factor in determining the severity of an injury in a rear-end collision. One of the contributing lawyers to this publication shared the following story.

"As a young lawyer I represented a couple in their 20's who were occupants of a car struck while stopped at a traffic light. Damage to their vehicle was slight, and to the bumper of the semi-truck that hit them, barely visible. The husband was a large burly fellow and had no complaint of injury. The wife was petite and complained of a sore neck, headache, and nausea at the scene. The husband was aware they were going to be hit just a second before the truck hit them and braced for the impact. The wife had no notice and was looking out the side window at a display in one of the stores [head rotated]. The claims adjuster convinced me that since the husband wasn't injured the wife couldn't have been hurt too badly. We settled the case for what was considered a fair value for a garden variety whiplash case. Ten years elapse and I bump into the wife in a store. It was a very upsetting experience. She had the same symptoms as when the case settled. She was in chronic pain, especially following any physical activity. There had been no intervening incidents which would have caused or contributed to her medical situation. It was then I realized there could be a lot more to these rear-end fender benders than originally thought".

For the difference in the potential for injury between men and women in a rear-end collision, see Myth No. 4: *Men and women are equally at risk to suffer whiplash injury in a rear impact collision.*

Two other factors contributing to the likelihood of occupant injury are occupant weight and occupant height.

"In general, smaller occupants are more likely to incur injuries than heavier persons because it takes more force to accelerate a larger occupant. It is evident in the crash literature that size may dictate occupant dynamics in a crash. The smaller-sized occupant will have higher head injury levels as the result of having less body mass and will incur less belt stretch and higher head acceleration. Additionally, if the shoulder harness for the small occupant is positioned close to the neck, the injury level will be greater. Smaller occupants will often have their seats positioned closer to the windshield or steering wheel than their larger counterparts, resulting in a higher incidence of chest impacts onto the steering wheel and dash." [18]

"Taller occupants have a higher risk of incurring neck injury in rear-end crashes due to the increased likelihood of having their head restraints positioned abnormally low, when compared to shorter occupants." [19]

A review of the section on head restraints and ramping (page 47) will be helpful in demonstrating why taller occupants are at greater risk of neck injury.

5. **AGE OF OCCUPANT:** The age of the vehicle occupant can also be a key factor in determining how severe the injury may be. The medical research has shown tolerance to impact in rear-end collisions decreases in occupants over the age of 50. Injury to occupants over the age of 65 results in substantially poorer prognosis. Older victims are more prone to injury because:

- Decreased back extensor strength (BES). A Mayo Clinic study concluded that women had a 50.4% decrease in their BES values from the fourth to the fifth decades. Men had a 64% loss of BES from the fourth to the ninth decades.

- Sarcopenia, or loss of skeletal muscle mass and strength, progresses with aging. By age 60, the prevalence of sarcopenia may be as high as 30%. The loss of voluntary maximal muscle strength in the seventh- and eighth-decades declines about 20% to 40% in males and females.

- Age is more significant than velocity in rear-end collision injury outcome.

- Decreased reserve capacity, decreased bone strength, decreased organ sinew, less adaptable brain tissue, and decreased blood vessel flexibility.

- Decreased intracellular fluid volume and decreased brain weight.

- Decreased brain size, primarily because of extracellular fluid loss, and decreased nerve conduction velocity. The connective tissues have increased density and decreased water as one ages.

- There is strong evidence there is also decreased capacity for repair, with lesser traumas being more difficult to heal.

- Older people also have less effective homeostatic mechanisms, which may increase their vulnerability to the environment. The negative balance between synthesis and degradation may change the metabolic balance of youth.

- Other changes may include decreased strength and speed of muscle contraction, and decreased numbers of functional motor units.

- Decreased tissue elasticity, calcification of tendons and ligaments, increased fibrous tissue, and generalized weakening of osseous and ligamentous structures.

"Older patients have slower rates of nerve regeneration. For the elderly, neck injury can be profoundly serious. The degenerative spine is biomechanically 'stiffer', behaving more like a single long bone than like a set of articulating structures. Deforming forces are less evenly dissipated, and more damage is done." [20]

Infants and young children [age 10 and younger] are also at a much higher risk for injury in a rear-end collision incident. Proportionately, the head of an infant or young child is much larger than their body.

"A heavy head on a small body results in high torques being applied to the neck and, consequently, a high susceptibility to flexion/extension injuries. The cervical musculature of a child is not fully developed, and the lax ligaments allow a significant degree of spinal mobility. Coupled with the fact the facet joints at C1 to C3 are nearly horizontal for the first several years of life allows for subluxations at relatively little force. Because of the larger [proportionately] head, the fulcrum of cervical movement is located higher in young children, putting them at a much higher risk for neck injury than a mature adult." [21]

7. **PRE-EXISTING COMPLICATING MEDICAL CONDITIONS:** The physical state of the occupant prior to the rear-end collision plays a significant role in the extent of injury and recovery outcome. In general, those occupants who are very athletic and have good muscle tone, flexibility, and endurance will recover faster and have fewer residual problems after the repair process. Nevertheless, even athletes may have difficulty or inability returning to pre-injury athletic skill levels after a car collision. The person who exhibits good overall physical condition, however, will have a higher tolerance to injury. Thus, higher speeds or greater acceleration forces are required to cause serious injury. This means that in a car with multiple occupants, if one of the occupants is in much better physical condition, he/she may not be injured while other occupants are injured. Sedentary persons tend to have less muscle mass, have less strength, and a lowered threshold for injury than their athletic counterpart, and are therefore at greater risk for injury, given the same crash circumstances.

Vehicle occupants involved in a rear-end collision with clinically significant pre-existing medical conditions may have more severe injuries, slower recovery times, and a much poorer prognosis.

If the occupant had a pre-existing degenerative spinal disease, even minor trauma from a rear-end collision can lead to serious spinal cord injury.

> *"Occupants whose spinal joints had degenerative joint changes before a M.I.S.T. type incident may incur more severe injuries and report more residual problems than those without degenerative joint changes."* [22]

Several studies concluded a pre-existing arthritic cervical spine would cause a minor impact collision to result in more serious injury than the same amount of force would create in the absence of arthritis. Degenerative diseases of the spine predispose the occupant to injury. Mild neck injuries in occupants having spondylosis may give rise to more serious injuries with lingering life-long symptoms.

IN SUMMARY

MYTH NO. 2: *The injury is a simple strain or sprain, and like a sprained ankle, will heal in 6-12 weeks.*

There are several key points related to the second myth. Let's start with definitions:

> **Soft Tissue:** muscles, ligaments, tendons, connecting tissues and nerves.
>
> **Sprain:** soft tissue is torn or ruptured.
>
> **Strain:** soft tissue is stretched beyond normal limits.
>
> **Extension:** Movement of the head and neck to the rear.
>
> **Flexion:** Movement of the head and neck forward.
>
> **Hyper:** Beyond the normal range of motion.

Acceleration may cause a strain or sprain injury through hyperextension and/or hyperflexion.

There are six factors that determine the severity of injury:

> 1. Force of Impact;
>
> 2. Occupant Awareness;
>
> 3. Position of Head at Impact;
>
> 4. Gender and Physical Build;
>
> 5. Age; and,
>
> 6. Pre-Existing Medical Condition.

CHECKLIST—MYTH NO. 2

1. Was the occupant aware of the impending collision?

2. Was the occupant's head rotated at the moment of impact?

3. Was the occupant seatbelt restrained at the moment of impact?

4. Was the occupant physically larger or smaller; man or woman; young or old?

5. Did the occupant have any pre-existing medical conditions?

Myth No. 3

The victim did not complain of pain at the scene of the incident (or to the investigating police officer or the emergency room personnel at the hospital) so if there was an injury, it must be slight.

This is one of the most common misconceptions about rear-end collision injuries—the delay in onset of symptoms. Before looking at the medical evidence which supports symptoms appearing 12–48 hours post incident, consider the following analogous situation. You are 40 years old and employed as a data analyst, meaning most of your day is spent looking at a computer screen. You are almost always tired at the end of the day and seldom exercise. It's a glorious Saturday fall afternoon. You are having friends over to watch your college alma mater battle their bitter rival that evening. To get in the mood an hour-long game of touch football breaks out at the local park across the street from your home. The adrenal is pumping as you catch a pass for the winning touchdown. Back at home watching the game that evening you are congratulating yourself on still "having it", shades of those glory days in high school. Sunday morning dawns and you realize you have a few stiff muscles as you head for the shower, but nothing a few Ibuprofen won't handle. It's Monday morning when you can hardly get out of bed that you realize you are in some serious pain. Rather than hobble into the office, you, the mighty weekend warrior, call in sick—36 hours after the touch football game.

The onset of pain may occur within 12 hours of the incident, or it may be delayed several days. Most victims feel the gradual intensity of pain developing for several days following the rear-end collision event.

"A delay in the onset of symptoms of several hours after impact is characteristic of whiplash injuries. Most patients feel little or no pain for the first few minutes after the injury; symptoms gradually intensify over the next days." [49]

"Although there are many factors as to why these symptom onset delays occur, one major factor is the spreading of post-traumatic edema. Gravity and the spread of bleeding and inflammation exudate along and between the myofascial plane will cause secondary swelling and inflammation. Using MRI to detect microscopic hemorrhage, one study found active bleeding in the deep anterior and posterior cervical muscles two to five days after injury." [23]

Q: What is the doctor who wrote this statement really saying? A: There is scientific or medical evidence to show continued bleeding in the injured soft tissue within the neck 2 to 5 days after the injury. The bleeding and inflammation (swelling) of the injured tissue causes pain, which is not always immediate at the time of injury.

Victims of rear-end collisions may also delay reporting an injury for these reasons:

1. The initial pain was not severe.

2. They attempted to resolve the pain at home with over the counter medication.

3. A doctor, family or friends said the injury would resolve itself.

4. The victim was suffering from post-traumatic anxiety.

5. The victim had more pressing priorities, like having the car repaired so they could get to work.

Priorities often determine the time for seeking treatment.

Generally, it is a good idea for the victim to keep a diary of all physical complaints following the rear-end collision incident, noting the time of onset of symptoms, type of symptoms and a scale of pain from 1 to 10, with 10 being the greatest pain imaginable.

"Particular neurologic symptoms and signs, such as early onset of headache and neck pain, and headache and neck pain intensity, may be indicators of a more severe injury. A short latency interval of symptoms seems to reflect a more severe injury." [24]

IN SUMMARY

MYTH NO. 3: *The victim did not complain of pain at the scene of the incident (or to the investigating police officer or the emergency room personnel at the hospital) so if there was an injury, it must be slight.*

The key point to remember regarding this myth is symptoms do not always appear immediately following a rear-end collision. Immediate symptoms and neck pain intensity may be indicators of a more severe injury. The medical literature states symptoms from rear-end collisions generally appear within 72 hours. It is important to note symptoms of a TMJ injury or a mild traumatic brain injury may not be recognized as such until months after the collisions. Why? Because the painful symptoms of other injuries may mask the symptoms of a TMJ or mild TBI injury. To learn more about TMJ and TBI injuries be sure to read pages 55-64.

CHECKLIST—MYTH NO. 3

1. When did you first notice pain from the rear-end collision?

2. Describe in detail, including location and severity. *Write it down in a journal.*

3. *Keep a daily log of symptoms in the journal*, noting how it affects your ability to work, play, relax and sleep.

MYTH NO. 4

Men and women are equally at risk to suffer whiplash injury in a rear impact collision.

It has been conclusively shown over the past fifty years, in both peer reviewed medical journal articles and scientific studies, women are twice as likely as men to suffer cervical injuries in a rear-end collision.

> *"An automotive study of 15,000 occupants found that in rear collisions, 42% of the women had cervical injuries, compared to 21% for men."* [50]

> *"Women have a significantly increased risk for whiplash injuries following a rear-end automobile collision."* [25]

- Females tend to drive smaller vehicles than males, resulting in a greater acceleration when impacted by a larger vehicle, and a greater likelihood of an impact with interior structures in the occupant compartment.
- Females tend to sit closer to the steering wheel, increasing the likelihood of impact.

- Generally, females have smaller and longer necks than males, which allows for higher acceleration of the head. As a group, females have less muscle strength in the cervical spine.

- In a comparison study of cadavers, it was found:

  "that females have less cartilage thickness in the facet joints than males, which can expose the underlying adjacent subcondral bone to direct stress during traumatic loading. Further, there are significantly greater segmental angles in the cervical spine, making female occupants more susceptible to injury." [26]

- Females tend to weigh less than males, making the seatback less likely to break in a rear-end crash, which results in a higher frequency of neck injuries.

- Females are more likely to have an improperly positioned shoulder harness. Smaller women [in the 10th percentile] are more likely to have the shoulder harness positioned directly against their neck; and, those with larger breasts may have the belt placed behind their back due to the discomfort.

In Summary

Myth No. 4: *Men and women are equally at risk to suffer whiplash injury in a rear impact collision.*

Women are twice as likely to be injured in a rear-end collision as men. Just because a male occupant was not injured in the rear-end collision does not mean a female occupant in the same vehicle was not injured.

Myth No. 5

The victim's soft tissue injuries have continued to improve for 12 months, post rear-end collision. In another few months, he/she will be fully recovered.

To address this myth, it is necessary to understand how the healing process for strain/sprain injuries occur. The healing process for soft tissue injuries occurs in three phases.

1. **The Acute Inflammatory Phase:** It is during this phase that hemorrhage from the injured tissue occurs with all the classical characteristics of an acute inflammatory response, namely swelling, redness, warmth, and pain. Depending on the severity of the injury, this phase may last for up to 72 hours.

2. **The Regeneration Phase:** *"Much of the credit for regeneration is given to the fibrocytes which are responsible for the secretion of collagen. The collagen glues, as they are sometimes referred to, help to attach the torn or injured tissues together. This phase lasts approximately 6–8 weeks."* [27]

To better understand the preceding medical journal quote, imagine two dry popsicle sticks. You wish to attach them to each other without nails, screws, or tape. What do you use? Elmer's glue. Collagen glues are the body's Elmer's glue, but unlike the one-time application of Elmer's, the body's collagen glues are being applied to the injured tissue during the entire 6–8 weeks of the Regeneration Phase of healing.

3. **THE REMODELING PHASE:** *"It is during this phase that the collagen glues, which play an important role in the tissue regeneration, are now remodeled on a more organized manner so as to resemble the tissue prior to injury. This phase* **may take as long as one year** *from the date of occurrence or onset of injury to be complete."* [28]

The application of the collagen glues continue as the soft tissue is gradually remodeled to as close as possible the shape and condition it was in before the injury. Depending on the severity of the injury, this could take 12 months.

"Not only do significant numbers of whiplash victims have persistent symptoms beyond a year, there is evidence some will have symptoms that worsen over time. Two separate studies conclude that 23% to 28% of whiplash victims will have worsening symptoms than those exhibited at the one-year anniversary of the rear-end collision." [29]

It is the opinion of the author of this publication that a victim of a rear-end collision should not attempt to negotiate a settlement with an insurance company until a minimum of six months has elapsed from the date of the collision, and then only if the victim is completely symptom free. Symptoms persisting one-year post collision warrant a follow-up examination by a doctor.

On a cautionary note, it is recommended that any rear-end collision victim, or any person affected by a rear-end collision, such as a spouse, parent or relative, read the chapter commencing at page 55 with an eye to understanding the symptoms of a closed head injury, or mild traumatic brain injury. It is estimated 80% of rear-end collision victims that suffer a closed head injury are never diagnosed, or treated, and go through life, along with their loved ones, wondering what has happened and why they are no longer the person they were before. Often times the incident creating this transformation of character is not considered—the causal connection of the injury with an apparent minor vehicle collision not being made.

IN SUMMARY

MYTH NO. 5: *The victim's soft tissue injuries have continued to improve for 12 months, post rear-end collision. In another few months, he/she will be fully recovered.*

Following soft tissue injury, the body goes through three stages of healing, which may take up to a year. Settlement with the auto insurance company for personal injuries should not occur until the victim is symptom free or has reached maximum medical improvement. At the earliest, at least six months should elapse from the date of the rear-end collision; or, if very minor symptoms, until all symptoms are gone. Whiplash injuries may continue to be symptomatic for up to 12 months; and, any symptom lingering after the 12-month mark should be considered permanent [see page 43]. Again, the victim, or those concerned with the victim's status, should read pages 55-64 to make certain the victim has not suffered a TMJ or TBI injury.

MYTH NO. 6

Permanent injuries from a whiplash injury are rare.

Permanent injuries from whiplash are common. Approximately 45% of whiplash victims have some nature of permanent symptoms and disability, with symptoms lasting two years or more. Not all the symptoms will be debilitating; many are simply aggravating, akin to having a pebble in your shoe. It may not have a lot of effect unless you are going on a hike, then it is very problematic. The same can be said for many types of whiplash related injuries—they are not problematic all the time. But, if there is yard work to be done, something to be lifted overhead, a physical activity [work or play] that never bothered the injured victim before, now the victim experiences pain. These limitations alter the way life is lived, and often result in a downward spiral of lessened physical activities of all kinds.

The majority of soft tissue injuries are usually stable and resolved within 12 months. The evaluation of permanency can then be made at that time. Mild injuries require one to six months to reach maximum recovery—nearly all of which result in complete recovery. Moderate injuries require six to nine months to reach maximum recovery—half of which result in some degree of permanent disability. Severe injuries require nine to twelve months to reach maximum recovery and the majority will have some degree of permanent disability. The medical profession uses the term "Maximum Medical Improvement" (MMI) to designate when a patient has reached the end of recovery. MMI means the patient is static and stable and is not expected to improve or show a decrease in improvement, plus or minus 3%, in the foreseeable future. In other words, MMI is the most one can hope for.

The truth of the matter regarding healing is this: If the victim of a rear-end collision is still having soft tissue symptoms and pain a year, or more, after the incident, the prognosis is not good. Here are reasons for this poor prognosis.

1. Repaired soft tissue is not as elastic nor resilient as its pre-injury state.

2. Ligament and tendon repair tend to be slower than muscle injuries primarily because of less blood flow; and, they are generally accompanied by more scarring than muscle tissue repair. There is a tendency for these tissues to over heal and create more scar tissue. This is largely due to a poorer vascular supply.

3. Soft tissue healed by scar are weaker than normal tissue, thus allowing for an increased susceptibility to pain and further injury.

4. The replacement of normal ligamentous tissue by fibrotic tissue sets the stage for a stiffer and more rigid joint, this resulting in joint and tissue hypomobility [not as flexible].

5. There is an increased amount of friction between poorly healed muscular tissue and the muscular tissue found directly adjacent [perineural fibrosis].

"The fibrosis scarring in or near the joint capsule can occur, limiting the range of motion of that particular joint. This can permanently interfere with the injured areas' daily musculoskeletal functions." [30]

"A seventeen-year study of 121 whiplash patients found one-half continuing to suffer with residual complaints, including neck pain, radiating pain, and headaches." [51]

"A study initiated by the World Health Organization and the United Nations reviewed 226 medical and scientific journal papers, with 47 of those specifically dedicated to Whiplash Associated Disorders (WAD) and found that 50% of WAD cases will continue to have symptoms at one year." [52]

IN SUMMARY

MYTH NO. 6: *Permanent injuries from a whiplash injury are rare.*

If the whiplash victim has reached maximum medical improvement, as determined by the treating physician, and still has symptoms, the injury is to be considered permanent. Even small permanent impairments, like the pebble in the shoe example, can alter one's approach to life—normal activities of daily living, work and leisure activities and hobbies that were previously enjoyed are now compromised.

MYTH NO. 7

When seat belt restrained and with a properly positioned head restraint or a high seat back, it is impossible for a whiplash injury to occur.

This myth is not even remotely true, having been soundly disproved by science and medical literature over the past 35 years. When properly positioned, seat belts reduce the serious nature of injury, specifically fatalities caused by vehicle occupants striking structures within the vehicle or being ejected from the vehicle. But, seat belts increase the incidence of cervical strain/sprain injuries. Wearing a seat belt is a risk factor for whiplash because the three-point seat belt prevents the torso from rebounding off the seat back. Instead, the body is held against the seat back and the head and neck are catapulted forward during the flexion portion of acceleration. One shoulder is pinned against the seat back causing a rotation of the head and neck in the direction of the restrained shoulder. This rotation action can exceed the normal range of cervical motion, resulting in the stretching and tearing of soft tissue on the unrestrained side of the neck.

"In fact, with retrained occupants, the seat belt is responsible for generating more injuries than any other contact source within the vehicle. The majority of these injuries are the product of the belt system operating in the manner in which it is designed, i.e., preventing an occupant contacting other structures within the vehicle." [31]

A properly positioned head restraint can be effective in preventing cervical injury in a rear-end collision. However, *"only 25% of adjustable head restraints are properly positioned."* The headrest should be at least as high as the level of the ears, and not further than two inches from the back of the head. If the headrest is positioned too low, or if the distance from the back of the head exceeds two inches, the headrest will act as a fulcrum in a rear-end collision and accentuate the injury. This phenomenon is known as "ramping". Ramping is caused by the combination of the rear impact and a slightly inclined seat back. It is the upward motion of the occupant in a struck vehicle immediately following impact. When this occurs, the head/neck complex may no longer be protected by the head restraint, which may then act as a fulcrum, increasing forces on the cervical spine. When the impact occurs from the rear, the vehicle tends to lift in the front, which lowers the seat 2-3 inches. The force of the collision, combined with the forward momentum, causes the occupant to "ride up" the seat back. Note the middle and lower illustrations on the following page.

Proper Head-Rest

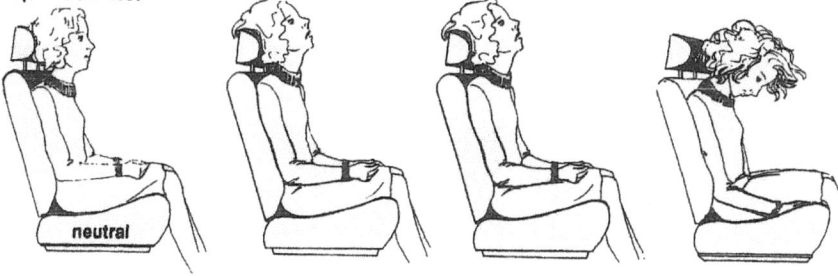

neutral

Low Head-Rest

neutral

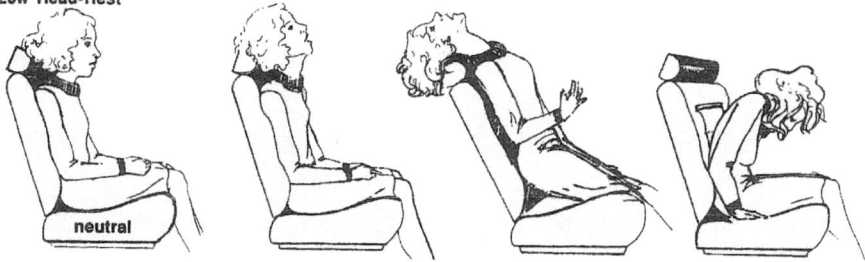

Absent Head-Rest

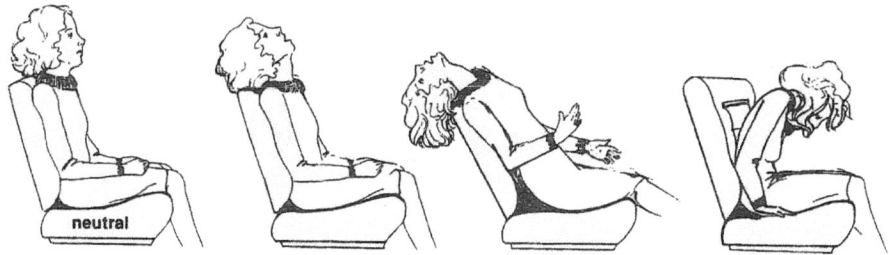

neutral

49

In Summary

Myth No. 7: *When seat belt restrained and with a properly positioned head restraint or a high seat back, it is impossible for a whiplash injury to occur.*

Wearing a seat belt is always a good idea as it protects the occupant from life threatening injuries in an auto collision, especially those injuries caused by occupant contact within the vehicle with a hard surface, such as a steering wheel or windshield. However, seat belts also may cause injury to the neck and back as the torso is restrained when the head and neck snap forward and rotate toward the restrained shoulder. This can also be a factor in closed head injuries (see page 55). A properly positioned head rest will protect an occupant from a hyperextension whiplash injury. An improperly positioned head rest will increase the likelihood of injury through the phenomenon of "ramping".

CHECKLIST—Myth No. 7

1. Was the injured occupant wearing a seat belt at the moment of the rear-end collision?

2. Was there a head restraint, and if so, was it properly positioned?

MYTH NO. 8

A whiplash injury does not affect a person's low back.

This is a classic example of the misinformation auto insurance adjusters are taught. The medical evidence gathered over a 40-year period from the 1980s to the present day shows that injury to the thoracic and lumbar spine occurred in 34% to 42% of all whiplash victims. The same mechanisms which cause cervical injury also cause injury to the low back: strain/sprain of the ligaments and soft tissue of the low back; nerve root entrapment; microfractures; and injury to joint capsules, especially those deep within the spinal structure. To briefly recap, the injury occurs within 'the blink of an eye' before the body has a chance to protect itself. The force applied to the neck and head most often exceeds the force and rate of acceleration applied to the vehicle occupant's low back (crack the whip example). But, the force which causes soft tissue to rupture and tear in the cervical region is sufficient to cause stretching and tearing in the soft tissue of the low back. This is even more evident in situations where ramping occurs, as the vertebrae in the low back are compressed as the torso rides up the seat back.

A study done in the year 2000 of 353 patients exposed to rear impacts found:

> *"53% initially complained of low back pain. After two years 40.5% had continued complaints of low back pain."* [32]

The authors of another study reviewed 6,481 auto insurance claims that were treated or filed within thirty days and looked at pain distribution. The study noted 80% posterior neck pain, 72% head pain, and *60% lumbar pain.* [33]

IN SUMMARY

MYTH No. 8: *A whiplash injury does not affect a person's low back.*

Approximately 50% of persons involved in a rear-end collision will have complaints of a low back injury.

MYTH NO. 9

The victim is trying to get a big settlement for a minor injury. Once compensated, the symptoms and pain will go away.

In 1961 Dr. Henry Miller concluded from a study of 200 head injury patients that 24% were suffering from psychoneurotic complaints with no organic basis. When all but four of the 45 victims involved in litigated cases returned to work, he concluded that settlement of the claim was the primary factor in their return to work. The auto insurance industry was quick to latch onto this report, and along with statements that most claimants are not hurt but are trying to defraud the auto insurance companies, denied many legitimate claims. As previously noted, the 3,000,000 rear-end collision cases reported annually represent a significant sum of money, even for insurance companies.

Dozens of subsequent peer reviewed medical studies from 1965 to the present have documented two very important facts. Dr. Miller's study was statistically invalid because it was a small subset of victims selected from over 4,000 patients, thus representing only 1% of the patients in the study; and, the treatment outcome was no different in the litigation and non-litigation groups of patients studied. Numerous studies have shown that injured persons continue to have physical changes even after litigation is concluded.

> *"The simplistic notion of financial gain as the all-important motive is not borne out by follow-up studies of patients when there is no further prospect of monetary reward from continuing disability."* [34]

> *"In a study of 102 whiplash victims, it was found that all litigating patients were still symptomatic 2 to 2 ½ years post collision, when the average time of settlement was 9 months."* [35]

> *"The vast majority of patients file claims because they are truly injured and wish compensation. In a system of tort law in which another party is responsible for the whiplash injury, this is exactly the expected result. By becoming involved in litigation, however, the victim can be further victimized by unsympathetic family members, physicians, employers, agents of insurance companies, and plaintiff attorneys who each have their own agenda. The evidence indicates that most patients who are still symptomatic when litigation is completed are not cured by a verdict. The end of litigation does not signal the end of symptoms for many patients. The patients who exaggerate or malinger are in a distinct minority."* [36]

In Summary

Myth No. 9: *The victim is trying to get a big settlement for a minor injury. Once compensated, the symptoms and pain will go away.*

The overwhelming majority of persons who file claims for injuries caused by the negligence of another are not "cured by a verdict or settlement". These victims simply want to be made whole and be returned to their same physical / mental condition before the collision.

MYTH NO. 10

Closed head injuries, or 'mild' traumatic brain injuries, do not occur in minor vehicle damage rear-end collisions.

*** CRITICAL INFORMATION ***

The information provided in this publication, to this point, has been important for the auto injured to understand injury can occur in a low-speed rear-end collision; and, injury may have long term implications, even though the injured area is classified as "soft tissue".

What is even more important, and the single most important piece of information in this publication, is this: ***It is possible for an occupant to sustain a closed head injury—a mild traumatic brain injury (TBI)—in a rear-end collision.***

The definition of a mild traumatic brain injury, or closed head injury, which may occur in a rear-end collision is defined as: ***An injury to the brain without a breach of the skull or the brain's surrounding tissues by a penetrating object***. In other words, it is an injury to the brain without the skull being split open and the brain exposed. Sometimes it is described as a concussion which may, or may not, include a loss of consciousness. It may occur without the head striking the interior of the vehicle. It can result from a low speed rear-end collision as the brain is subjected to the same forces of acceleration/deceleration and rotation previously discussed.

A contributing author shared stories from clients that illustrate the limitations and frustrations common to mild TBI victims. One client, Kenny, a father to five pre-college aged children, was hit in an intersection by an inattentive young driver. He did not strike his head or lose consciousness. He suffered neck pain and an immediate headache. He was examined at the Emergency Room, given pain medication and told his symptoms would resolve in a few weeks. His wife knew there was more to the injury a week later when Kenny called from the grocery store, not because he had forgotten what he was to buy (his wife had given him a list), but because he could not remember how to get back home (where they had lived for 18 years).

Another client, Bob, had been employed as a data analyst for 14 years with the same company. Following his incident, he had to have assistance every day to log into a new system on his computer. He simply could not remember how to activate the program. He was able to perform most of the tasks he had done previously, but new processes and procedures were more than he could handle. He was terminated six months after his incident.

Sally was a 42-year-old bright, vivacious, and witty schoolteacher. She was usually the center of attention and life of the party at social situations. The year following her incident she became increasingly depressed and withdrawn. Her inability to remember punch lines and key bits of information crucial to her stories led her to believe she was losing her mind. She became increasingly withdrawn and embarrassed at hearing comments by her fellow teachers, "What's up with Sally?" She did not associate her issues with the seemingly minor fender bender a year earlier.

Kay graduated from law school at the top of her class with an offer to clerk for a Federal Judge upon passing the Bar Exam. While studying for the Bar Exam the summer following graduation her small compact car was rear-ended at a stop sign by a fully loaded semi-truck. There was minimal damage to her car and no damage to the semi, though the force of impact was enough to knock her car through the intersection. Kay subsequently failed the Bar Exam three times. When interviewed as a prospective client three years later the Statute of Limitations for a claim against the semi-truck's insurance company had expired. No one in the medical or legal field had suggested to Kay that her mental issues may have been caused by a TBI related to the rear-end collision. At last report Kay was working as a clerk at a convenience store.

The incidence of closed head injuries occurring in the three million rear-end collisions annually is unknown. It is estimated 80% of all closed head injuries are either not diagnosed, or are misdiagnosed, by both the medical and legal professions. These victims go through life with their injury never diagnosed, never treated, and never compensated.

A 2001 study of 639 patients with a mild head injury found the most common complaints included: *"fatigue, headache, dizziness, irritability, sleep disturbance, poor concentration and poor memory, in that order."* [37]

Following is a checklist of symptoms attributable to closed head injuries caused by a rear-end collision.

Headache	Dizziness
Impaired Concentration	Fatigue
Speech and Communication Problems	Depression
Anger and/or Frustration	Anxiety
Difficulty Sleeping	Confusion
Difficulty with Organizational Tasks	Difficulty on the Job
Personality Change	Memory Impairment
Impaired Perception	Decreased Language Skills
Loss of Executive Skills	Inappropriate Behavior
Relationship Problems	Denial Anything is Wrong
A Feeling of Losing Their Mind	Irritability
Memory Difficulties	Lack of Patience

Distrust of Legal Profession, Insurance Companies	Distrust of Physicians
Mood Swings	Reduced Attention Span
Loss or Absence of Smell or Taste	Sensitive to Noise or Light

DIAGNOSIS AND TREATMENT FOR MILD TBI

An injury to the brain is obviously the most serious of non-fatal injuries to be suffered in a rear-end collision. Diagnosis and treatment are complex and require specialists. These issues are more fully addressed in "Whiplash & Traumatic Brain Injury—An Epidemic", soon to be available on Amazon. Review the symptoms listed, and if there is a concern you, or someone you care about, is suffering from a mild traumatic brain injury, consider ordering this book. Another option is to schedule an appointment with your primary care provider and share with him/her the symptoms you are experiencing and your concerns. With a greater public awareness of brain injuries through sports, especially football, many health care providers are more inclined to give credence and attention to claims of brain injury.

IN SUMMARY

MYTH NO. 10: *Closed head injuries, or 'mild' traumatic brain injuries, do not occur in minor vehicle damage rear-end collisions.*

Closed head injuries can occur in even minor collisions. It is estimated 80% of mild TBI injuries from rear-end collisions are never diagnosed, treated, or compensated. Since the brain controls every function of the body, the mildest of brain injuries will impact some of the body's functions. If the auto injured victim has a majority of the symptoms noted above, it is highly recommended a timely and extensive inquiry be made to determine whether a mild TBI has occurred.

CHECKLIST—MYTH NO. 10

1. Review Checklist Items for the first three Myths.

2. Was there a head strike?

3. Did the victim lose consciousness?

4. Does the victim have more than half of the symptoms noted in this chapter?

MYTH NO. 11

TMJ (Temporomandibular Joint) injuries do not occur in minor vehicle damage rear-end collisions.

The Temporomandibular Joint is located at the back of the jaw. It acts like a sliding hinge, connecting the jawbone to the skull. There is one such joint on each side of the jaw. TMJ disorders can cause pain in the jaw joint, in the muscles that control jaw movement, in the neck structure and in the head in the form of debilitating headaches.

In whiplash injuries, the head is thrown backward and then violently whipped forward, tearing muscles, stretching ligaments and occasionally herniating cervical vertebral discs. These same forces act on the mandible and the TMJ. When the mandible is thrown forward, the capsular and discal ligaments are stretched, compromising the stability of the joint.

A variety of symptoms may be linked to TMJ disorders. The most common symptom is pain in the chewing muscles and/or jaw joint. Other symptoms include:

- radiating pain in the face, jaw, or neck,

- jaw muscle stiffness,
- limited movement or locking of the jaw,
- dizziness,
- vertigo,
- painful clicking, popping, or grating in the jaw joint when opening or closing the mouth,
- a change in the way the upper and lower teeth fit together, and
- headaches.

One of the contributing authors shared this client story. "It was a late afternoon and I received a call from a new client in such severe pain she was considering suicide. Her headache was such she could hardly see; and as a further insult, she could not eat because it hurt to chew. She still had all the other symptoms from the incident the week before, but the headache had gotten so much worse and now her jaw was popping every time she opened her mouth. That casually mentioned symptom tipped me off she might have a TMJ injury. Frankly, I hadn't considered it before. I was able to get her an appointment that afternoon with an oral surgeon who diagnosed the TMJ injury and was able to have a Gelb splint for her the next morning. Her pain relief was almost immediate. I have been on her Christmas card list since that day."

Even though the signs and symptoms of TMJ are present, they are often masked by more painful cervical injuries and go unnoticed. Headaches are the most common single symptom of TMJ derangement following a rear-end collision. The headache may be temporal (on either side of the eye at the temple) or occipital (at the base of the skull) in location and may vary in intensity throughout the day. The victim is generally unaware of the relationship between the clicking and popping of the jaw and the headache. Other symptoms of TMJ include a "fullness" in the ears, neck and shoulder pain, and a sharp pain behind the eye.

The prevalence of TMJ injuries is noted in these medical journal articles. In an eighteen-month Canadian study concluded in 2007, it was found: *"there is reduced and/or painful jaw movement occurring in 15.8% of people suffering Whiplash Associated Disorders."* [38]

> *"Jaw symptoms are seldom reported during the acute phase after a whiplash trauma. Women more often than men develop jaw symptoms during the first year. Jaw symptoms and signs may develop also after low-speed impacts, especially after rear-end collisions. Jaw symptoms and signs should be observed after whiplash trauma, especially in those with headache, pronounced neck problems, cranial neck symptoms and post-traumatic stress."* [39]

The preceding study was conducted between 1997 - 2001 and found that 24% of persons involved in low-speed impacts had TMJ symptoms one-year post collision.

The Society of Automotive Engineers concluded a study in 1999 where reconstruction analysis of rear-end crashes showed 18% of occupants suffered TMJ injuries. [40]

In Summary

Myth No. 11: *TMJ (Temporomandibular Joint) injuries do not occur in minor vehicle damage rear-end collisions.*

An injury to the TMJ may result from a minor vehicle damage rear-end collision. Approximately one in five persons injured in a rear-end collision will suffer a TMJ injury. These injuries are often masked by the more obvious injury to the soft tissue of the neck and back. A TMJ injury can be extremely painful. The most common symptoms are clicking and popping in the jaw; and, headaches, often originating at the temple, behind the eye or at the base of the neck.

CHECKLIST—MYTH NO. 11

1. Does the injured victim have "clicking or popping" in the jaw?

2. Does the injured victim have headaches originating at the base of the neck, or in the temple region (feels like a nail being driven into the side of their head)?

3. Does the injured victim have pain originating behind the eye?

4. Does the injured victim have dizziness (vertigo), ringing in the ear (tinnitus) or a feeling of fullness in the ear?

ALTERNATIVE TREATMENT OPTIONS

This section is not intended as medical advice and should not be taken as such. It is information and knowledge to help you seek treatment for long-term results. In all instances it is best to consult with a licensed medical practitioner. Don't be afraid to ask questions of health care providers. Traditional western medical treatment typically provides pain relievers and muscle relaxants as the first response to a whiplash injury. That is acceptable during the first phase of healing, up to 72 hours. Keep in mind, however, pharmaceuticals are treating symptoms and not the cause of the problem. The auto injured victim should be aware there are alternative treatment options for "soft tissue" type injuries. Mobilization of the injured soft tissue is a sound medical principle in understanding why certain treatments may be more advantageous than others.

On page 39, Three Phases of Healing are discussed. It is the second phase, the Regeneration Phase, which is the motivator in seeking treatment following a rear-end collision. Treatment should be considered as soon as the Acute Inflammatory Phase [0-72 hours] has subsided. For the next 6–8 weeks the injured tissue is being 'remodeled' through secretion of collagen glues which attach the torn and injured tissues. It is important treatment be sought during this time, preferably as soon as is practicable, utilizing one, or more, of the treatments noted below.

Consider the following quotes from medical journal articles which emphasize mobilization of the injured soft tissue is required for best treatment results:

"Early mobilization was found to be superior to the standard therapy of neck collars and immobilization. Mobilization can be defined as low velocity passive movements within or at the limit of joint range of motion. The importance of mobilization cannot be understated. Clinical outcomes with manual therapy resulted in faster and more complete recovery." (41)

"The cumulative evidence suggests that prolonged periods of rest are detrimental to recovery from whiplash associated disorders. Cervical collars promote inactivity, which can delay recovery." (42)

"It has been shown that normal tension in healing muscles results in quicker and stronger repair. Excessive scar formation leaves a muscle weak, less elastic, less pliable, and often more sensitive. Immobilization, while beneficial early on in a muscle injury [Phase One], has detrimental effects when prolonged. Prolonged immobilization results in a weaker scar and a greater potential for re-injury. Normal tension in the healing muscle results in quicker and stronger repair." (43)

"Active intervention in patients with Whiplash Associated Disorders improves long-term prognosis. Treatments started within fourteen days following a motor vehicle collision, evaluated at six months and three years, found pain intensity and sick leave were significantly reduced as compared to standard intervention." (53)

The question then is: what type of therapeutic treatment(s) will provide *"normal tension"* and/or *"early mobilization"*? There are at least three forms of treatment that meet this standard. Each on their own can supply satisfactory results, but a combination of two or three will assist the auto injured victim in making the best recovery possible.

PHYSICAL THERAPY: *Physical therapy is for the restoration of movement and physical function impaired by injury, or disability, that utilizes therapeutic exercise, physical modalities (such as massage and electrotherapy), assistive devices, and patient education and training.* It includes the examination, treatment, and instruction of persons in order to detect, assess, prevent, correct, and limit physical disability and bodily malfunction caused by rear-end collisions. Physical therapy is generally prescribed by a medical doctor.

MASSAGE THERAPY: *Massage therapy is the scientific manipulation of the soft tissues of the body for the purpose of normalizing those tissues and consists of manual techniques that include applying fixed or movable pressure, holding, and/or causing movement of or to the body.* These effects can provide a number of benefits:

- Reduction of muscle tension and stiffness;
- Relief of muscle spasms;
- Greater flexibility and range of motion;
- Increase of the ease and efficiency of movement;
- Promotion of faster healing of soft tissue injuries;
- Reduction in pain and swelling of soft tissue injuries; and,
- Reduction in the formation of excessive scar tissue following soft tissue injuries

Massage therapy may be prescribed by a medical doctor, be a part of a physical therapy program or be independently sought out by the injured victim.

CHIROPRACTIC: *Chiropractic is a noninvasive therapy in which the misalignment of the spine and joints causing pain is manually adjusted to return the spinal vertebrae to their proper position in the spinal column.* Chiropractic is one of the most popular alternative therapies currently available for treatment of the auto injured. Chiropractors are the first health care provider in half of all rear-end collision cases. It has become a well-accepted treatment for acute pain and problems of the spine, including lower back pain and whiplash related injuries. Chiropractic comes from Greek words meaning "done by hand". It is grounded in the principle the body can heal itself when the skeletal system is correctly aligned, and the nervous system is functioning properly. The practitioner uses his or her hands or an adjusting tool to perform specific manipulations of the vertebrae. When these bones of the spine are not correctly aligned, a condition known as subluxation, nerve transmission is disrupted and causes pain in the neck and back, as well as other areas of the body. Chiropractic treatment carries none of the risks of surgical or pharmacologic treatment and can significantly shorten the healing process for injuries caused by a rear-end collision.

Often the chiropractor is the first health care provider a patient sees for his/her condition following a rear-end collision. The Center of Studies in Health Policy has stated the chiropractor is a primary care provider, considered a "gate keeper" when a patient enters the health care system. This includes diagnostic differentiation, assessment, treatment, and referral. [45]

The Insurance Research Council, citing data from 42,038 claims from twenty-two insurance companies, reported chiropractors see 41% of all personal injury auto claims for strain/sprain injuries. [44]

ADDITIONAL OPTIONS FOR PAIN RELIEF

There are a number of tried and proven techniques for resolving pain and muscle spasms without the necessity of medications. This section does not address pain medications or muscle relaxants except in the initial Acute Inflammatory Phase when they may be necessary to cope with the pain of injury. After the initial phase of healing, consideration should be given to other methods of dealing with pain.

ACUPUNCTURE: Acupuncture is one of the main forms of treatment in traditional Chinese medicine. It involves the use of sharp, thin needles inserted in the body at specific points. The World Health Organization (WHO) recommends acupuncture as an effective treatment for over forty medical problems, including pain from auto injuries. It is an effective and low-cost treatment for headaches and chronic pain associated with back injuries and whiplash. It is now widely recognized by doctors as effective for pain reduction.

WEIGHTED BLANKETS: What is a weighted blanket? Just what it says: a blanket filled with a substance to add weight to the blanket. The blanket should be about 10% of the person's body weight. A person weighing 150 pounds would select a blanket weighing 15 pounds. The underlying science on weighted blankets is "Deep Touch Pressure" (DTP). The idea behind a weighted blanket is the added weight makes the user feel as if they are receiving a gentle hug. It has been described as having a 'grounding feeling' on the body leading to an increased sense of relaxation.

Many whiplash victims have difficulty sleeping following injury due to pain, or the trauma of the event. Anything to enhance resting outside of a drug induced sleep should be considered. Studies have shown DTP increases the body's production of serotonin, a chemical in the body that promotes relaxation and reduces anxiety. DTP has also been shown to alleviate symptoms in people suffering from insomnia and chronic pain.

TENS UNIT: A transcutaneous electrical nerve stimulation (TENS) unit is a device that sends small electrical currents to targeted body parts to control pain signals in the body, creating temporary or permanent relief from pain. Some TENS units are designed for use in a hospital or healthcare facility and may be employed by a physical therapist or chiropractor. Others are safe for home use and can be purchased independently. Home use Tens units are generally battery-powered devices. Electrodes attached to the skin transmit electrical impulses, which produce a mild tingling or massaging sensation. Reasons for the effectiveness of this method include interruption of pain impulses from the periphery to the central nervous system; increased production of endorphins; and, improved blood supply to the affected part. Increased circulation encourages healing and helps reduce muscle spasm.

PROLOTHERAPY: Prolotherapy is a **non-surgical injection procedure used to relieve back and neck pain** by treating connective tissue injuries (ligaments and tendons) that have not healed by either rest or conservative therapy. A series of injections at the affected area promote a healing response in small tears and weakened tissue, alleviating the pain, and improving function. It is considered an alternative therapy for treating musculoskeletal pain, and in most instances the treatment is not covered by insurance. However, it has been shown to be effective in treating chronic pain victims when other forms of therapy or treatments have failed.

ESSENTIAL OILS AND OTHER SUPPLEMENTS: An essential oil is a concentrated hydrophobic liquid containing volatile chemical compounds from plants. Essential oils are also known as volatile oils, ethereal oils, or simply as the oil of the plant from which they were extracted, such as oil of clove. An essential oil is "essential" in the sense it contains the "essence of" the plant's fragrance—the characteristic fragrance of the plant from which it is derived. The term "essential" used here does not mean indispensable, as with essential amino acid or essential fatty acid, which are so called because they are nutritionally required by a given living organism.

The use of essential oils and other supplements are considered alternative methods of dealing with pain. There are many essential oils that can be used to block and/or relieve pain. However, the proper essential oil, in the proper preparation and presentation, is important. A trustworthy resource is "Essential Oils Pocket Reference, 8th Edition (2019)" published by Life Science Publishing.

Another excellent reference material is: "The Miracle of MSM: The Natural Solution for Pain" by Dr. Ronald Lawrence and Dr. Stanley Jacobs. Both books are available on Amazon.

Natural supplements to reduce inflammation include Turmeric and CoQ 10. These products are available in most grocery stores, drug stores and online. There are multiple brands to choose from in varying price ranges. These will most likely not be covered by insurance. The pain and inflammation reduction response time will vary by individual and product.

Selecting the Right Lawyer for Your Case

In all professions there are experts, or specialists, in every field. There are college professors teaching English Literature, with little understanding of Chemistry. There are physicians who operate on the brain, while others repair hernias and hemorrhoids. You will not learn much chemistry from the English Lit professor; and, which doctor would you want operating on your brain?

There are lawyers who draft wills and plan estates, lawyers who handle everything from Bankruptcy to DWI, and lawyers who represent those injured by the negligence of others. They are called Plaintiff Personal Injury Lawyers and that is who you want to hire. There are plaintiff personal injury lawyers who have represented the auto injured multiple times, even before a jury. There are those who advertise as personal injury lawyers and have never set foot in a courtroom. How do you know which lawyer to choose? It is an important decision. You have only one chance to settle your case and get it right. Once the case is settled and you have signed the Release Form, you can never go back and ask for more money. This is why it is so important to get it right. Choosing the right lawyer is your best start.

The best recommendation for a plaintiff Personal Injury [PI] Attorney is a referral from a former client the attorney has already successfully represented. Another good source of referrals for PI lawyers are your treating health care professionals. They usually know which lawyer does a good job representing their patients. If they don't have a referral, call the local BAR Association, and ask for the list of attorneys listing personal injury as their area of practice. The last person to call is the attorney with the flashy billboard or big Yellow Page ad.

When you have narrowed your choice to two or three, call the office and schedule an appointment, noting the subject matter of the appointment is to discuss a personal injury matter. Most personal injury law firms will give the initial interview an hour without charge. [FYI: If the initial interview does not take at least an hour, the attorney did not ask enough questions or elicit enough information. This is not the lawyer you want.] As a general rule of thumb, most PI lawyers operate on a contingency basis, being paid only for their time if the client makes a recovery from the negligent party. The fee may range from 25% - 33% of the settlement amount if the case is settled without filing a lawsuit, to 40% - 50% if the case is tried. The client is responsible for the costs of preparing, filing, and/or litigating the case. These fees and costs are usually advanced by the law firm and deducted from the settlement or verdict when the case resolves.

Generally, this is how your representation begins. The lawyer will have you sign a Fee Agreement and issue a Letter of Representation acknowledging he/she will be handling your case. If you don't have a signed Fee Agreement and a signed Letter of Representation from the lawyer, you do not have an attorney representing you. Be sure to retain a copy of both documents for your files.

The initial interview is actually two interviews. The lawyer is interviewing you to see if there is a case, and if so, if they are interested in pursuing the matter. You, as the injured victim, are interviewing the lawyer to see: 1) if they are competent; and, 2) if they are a good fit for you. Hiring the right lawyer for your case is important. It can make all the difference in whether you receive a settlement, and if so, the size of the settlement. Keep this in mind: most auto injured victims would rather have their health back than any sum of money.

The following questions are for the attorney in the initial interview and should be a determining factor in who you select to represent you.

- How long have you been in practice?
- Do you have an area of specialty?
- Have you ever tried a case to a jury? If so, how many?
- Have you ever tried a rear-end collision case? If so, what was the result?
- Will you explain how my injury occurred? [The lawyer should at least be familiar with the concepts explained earlier in this publication].
- What are my elements of damage? [Medical bills, loss of income, pain & suffering, and permanency of the injury, no matter how slight].
- Will you provide the name and phone number of other clients you have represented in similar cases?
- What is my case worth? [If the lawyer answers this question without having seen the medical records you need to leave—at once. Any lawyer that predicts the value of a case without having seen the medical records, AND before the auto injured victim has reached a static and stable medical condition and been released from medical care, is not competent to handle your case, or any PI case.]

If the lawyer passes these questions, ask yourself these two questions:

1. Do I have a good feeling about this lawyer?

2. Can I trust this lawyer with what I know now?

If you cannot answer both of those questions in the positive, keep looking.

Should I Attempt to Settle the Case Myself?

Whether to hire a lawyer or not is a question only you can answer. Some auto injured victims are perfectly capable of representing their own interests. Others may have been before the incident, but now find themselves at a disadvantage due to physical and/or mental impairments caused by the collision. Others are not comfortable with the thought of negotiating with an insurance company and need the voice and skill of an experienced legal advocate. If you are not sure if you should attempt to settle your own case, read on. Only the stout of heart and those determined to see justice done will have the wherewithal to see this journey through. For many, the tactics employed by the auto insurance industry will cause them to settle for far less than their injuries warrant. It is not an easy game to play, and as an inexperienced auto injured victim, you are not evenly matched with a claims adjuster who has handled hundreds, if not thousands, of these types of claims over the course of their career.

You have three things which set you apart from most auto injured victims. One, your knowledge of the mechanisms of injury and the potential seriousness of your injury level the playing field with the claims adjuster—*somewhat* [Review pages 9-64]. Two, the information in this chapter will give you an insight into tactics that may be employed in your dealings with a claims adjuster. Knowing how the process works and the tactics you will likely run into will also help level the field. Just knowing this information will alleviate much of the uncertainty and frustration associated with settling your own case. Finally, if you are unable to reach a fair and equitable settlement with the insurance company, you will be equipped with the knowledge of how to hire competent legal counsel [see page 73].

Several years ago, the Insurance Research Council came out with a stunning statistic. Whiplash victims who hired lawyers ended up with approximately One Thousand Dollars ($1,000.00) *less* than those who settled the case on their own. This can be attributed to two factors: 1) Not all lawyers are competent to represent whiplash cases; and, 2) Most personal injury lawyers work on a contingency basis. That is, they receive a percentage of the settlement or verdict amount when the case is resolved. The percentage may vary from 25% to 50%, depending on the nature and complexity of the matter; and, whether the case is litigated and/or appealed. The "normal" fee for personal injury cases not litigated is one-third (33%). Most personal injury law firms advance the reasonable costs of the case and recoup these costs at settlement or verdict. Reasonable costs may include postage, photocopies, charges for certified copies of medical records, accident reports, filing fees, etc. If you represent yourself, you will bear these expenses.

If you are still considering representing yourself, let's begin. There are three important issues in determining whether you have a case worth pursuing.

First, is there CLEAR LIABILITY? In other words, did you do anything to cause or contribute to the cause of the collision? Did you fail to yield at an intersection when you were required to? Did you pull out in front of another vehicle while entering traffic from an on-ramp? Did you pull off the shoulder of the road and stop for a necessary reason, *but* fail to completely clear the lane of traffic? Did you slam on the brakes to avoid hitting a squirrel when you knew (or should have known) there was a vehicle behind you? [Drivers of vehicles are to be aware of traffic, including vehicles following]. Slamming on the brakes to avoid hitting a child darting into the street or a person who stumbles into traffic is one thing and is always excusable. The size and nature of an animal in your lane of traffic makes it a case by case determination. Braking suddenly to avoid a 2,000-pound bull that would cause serious damage to your vehicle and potentially its occupants is excusable. Braking suddenly to avoid a squirrel could mean you are contributorily negligent, a fact the insurance adjuster will be certain to mention as they look for any reason to discount your claim. Sitting at a complete stop at a red light when another vehicle slams into the back your vehicle is an example of clear liability of the other person's negligence. If there is clear liability, proceed to the second issue. If not, it may be time to consider consulting with an attorney. *Just because liability is not clear does not mean you do not have a case.* What it does mean is it will take someone skilled in dealing with an auto insurance company to achieve a fair settlement.

Second, do you have INJURIES DIRECTLY ATTRIBUTABLE TO THIS INCIDENT? If you cannot document with medical reports your injury was either caused, *or a prior condition made worse*, by this incident, you have no case for a personal injury claim. You may still have a case for property damage to your vehicle and/or vehicle contents, but not for a personal injury. Caveat: If you had a pre-existing condition or injury, but were asymptomatic (had no symptoms at the time of the incident), and now you have pain and symptoms (as documented in the medical records), then you have a personal injury claim. If you had a pre-existing condition for which you were symptomatic (had symptoms related to the pre-existing condition) at the time of the incident, and those symptoms are now exacerbated (made worse), then you have a personal injury claim. As an example, let's assume you are recovering from back surgery three weeks before the rear-end collision. You still have lingering pain related to the surgery and physical limitations. Following the collision, you are incapacitated, and the pain is intense. You have a personal injury case if the medical records and the doctor's assessment note your present condition has worsened. Review this topic in sections "Pre-Existing Complicating Medical Conditions" (page 29) and "Permanency of Injury" (page 83).

Third, what type of INSURANCE COVERAGE is there? If the person driving the vehicle that collided with yours has insurance, it is likely an insurance claims adjuster for that company will call you for a statement, to assess the amount of damage to your vehicle and whether you have been hurt. If you have not heard from a claims adjuster within a week, use the information given to you at the scene of the collision, or from the police report, to contact either the insurance company or the person driving the vehicle that hit your vehicle. You should have already contacted your insurance company to inform them of the collision. They may be able to assist in contacting the adverse insurance company. *Review the telephone tips on pages 85-86 before calling the claims adjuster.*

Every state requires the owner of a vehicle to have liability insurance, at a minimum. Most states require proof of insurance before a person can purchase license tags for the vehicle. Occasionally it will happen an auto insurance policy will lapse for nonpayment and the owner of the vehicle will continue to drive. The problem arises when that driver causes an incident. If the person responsible for the incident does not have insurance coverage, all is not lost. Review the Declaration page of your auto insurance policy and determine if you have "Uninsured Motorist Coverage", often noted as UM Coverage, or UIM Coverage. In terms of settling your case this may be to your advantage. As an example, assume the negligent party, Ms. Brown, a 19-year-old college student, had insurance with

State Farm Insurance Company. If you were unable to settle with State Farm and were forced to bring a lawsuit, the named defendant would be Ms. Brown. The jury would never know State Farm was financially responsible for paying the verdict. The jury's sympathies could be with Ms. Brown and the verdict returned might not be fair.

On the other hand, assume Ms. Brown failed to pay her auto insurance premium and her policy with State Farm had lapsed. She has no insurance coverage. She is personally liable for any damage she may have caused by her negligence. Being a 19-year-old college student, she likely has no assets or the ability to pay for your injury. You are insured by Allstate Insurance Company and have Uninsured Motorist Coverage. You will be much more likely to settle with Allstate than with State Farm. Why? If the case does not settle, Allstate becomes the named defendant in the lawsuit. Juries are much more likely to award a fair settlement against a multi-billion-dollar insurance giant, than against some poor 19-year-old college student.

WHAT IS THE VALUE OF YOUR CASE? The value of your personal injury case hinges primarily on three factors: 1) your **medical records**; 2) whether there is a claim for **loss of income**; and, 3) the **permanency**, if any, **of the injury**. [*There is a fourth category typically discounted by claims adjusters, but it is very real to the auto injured victim. The category is referred to as "pain and suffering", and in addition to its namesake, includes mental and emotional duress, the inconvenience of visiting doctors and planning for all that entails (missing work, childcare arrangements, etc.)*]. Pertinent details for these categories follow:

MEDICAL RECORDS: It is important they be accurate and complete. To maximize your settlement, do the following:

1. Keep all scheduled medical appointments, if possible.

2. Be accurate in reporting how the injury occurred; and, your symptoms.

Do not overstate your pain levels or limitations. **Do not understate them either.** This is a common mistake for many injured victims, especially if there was only minor damage to the vehicle.

3. Explain to the treating physician and/or health care provider, *in detail*, how the injury is affecting your activities of daily living, i.e., it is difficult to clothe yourself, to go up and down stairs, to perform the requirements of your job, lifting an item weighing X pounds, sleeping soundly is a challenge, you are always tired and fatigued—whatever the impact has been on your 'normal' life, be sure to tell the medical personnel [with the expectation it will go in their medical records]. You also want to note how this injury has affected your ability to enjoy your family and any leisure time, hobbies, or pastimes you previously enjoyed, but which are now limited due to the injury. Keep a daily / weekly journal noting levels of pain and limitations of activities.

4. Finally, be aware the claims adjuster will request a Medical Authorization to gather your medical records for their file. Be careful to note the specific time period for which the authorization is valid. You may be giving permission for the adjuster to look at your medical records going back to childhood. Limit the authorization to those records relevant to your present claim. If you have questions about what is appropriate, consider retaining legal counsel.

LOSS OF INCOME: To prove a loss of income you must be able to document time off from work, or the manner in which the income was lost due to the incident and resulting injury. Be prepared to show income received the six months prior to the incident, and then for the months in which the loss of income is claimed. This can be accomplished through pay stubs, commission statements, transaction reports, etc. as your specific job situation provides. It is not uncommon for claims adjusters to also request copies of tax returns and an employment history. If litigation is filed, the defense is generally entitled to a few years tax returns and a fairly complete employment history. Since you are attempting to settle your case without litigation or hiring a lawyer, providing tax returns should not be necessary unless your claim for loss of income exceeds twelve months, and/or a claim for future loss of income. In either event, you may wish to consider retaining legal counsel at this point.

PERMANENCY OF INJURY: Peer reviewed medical journal articles note symptoms continuing for twelve months or more are considered permanent in nature. The journal articles also clearly state soft tissue which has suffered a strain/sprain injury will be more susceptible to injury in the future, from even a minor force. This susceptibility to future injury is permanent. Here are two important questions to ask your health care provider.

- Since it has now been twelve months from the date of my injury and I continue to have symptoms, do you consider this injury to be permanent?
- Am I more likely than not to be injured in the future at the same place as my present injury?

Should the physician answer one or both questions in the affirmative, ask him/her to note the same in the file, and then ask this question:

- Will I require future medical treatments for this injury, and if so, what do you recommend, and how often?

Ask the doctor to note this in the file as well.

If it has been a year or more since your injury, another technique that may be of value in your negotiations with the claims adjuster is the use of letters from family, friends, and co-workers. Generally this approach is best left with an attorney, but it may be helpful if the person writing the letter can detail how much the injury has impacted you AND they are willing to discuss the matter by phone (or in person) with the adjuster. Because you will most likely not be present when the phone call or visit with the author of the letter is made, you have no control over what is said. Claims adjusters can be very persuasive and skilled at asking questions that lead to an answer not favorable to your claim. The conversation may also be recorded, with a high possibility of it being damaging at trial. Unless you are confident of the person giving the statement, it is recommended you leave this approach to legal counsel.

THE DEMAND LETTER: Once you have been released by the treating health care physician, and/or the treating health care physician has stated you have reached maximum medical improvement, it is time to write the Demand Letter. Remember to ask the treating health care professional if you will require future periodic maintenance treatments, and if so, how often and how many.

A sample of the Demand Letter is included in the Appendix as Exhibit "A". This is a format which clearly identifies why you are entitled to a settlement. Modify it to conform to the facts of your case. In every case make sure the letter is typed, free from misspellings and grammatical errors, and contains all the records referenced in the letter. Since you may never meet the adjuster face to face, it is important the adjuster view the letter as coming from someone knowledgeable and efficient. Always request a time for a phone call in approximately two weeks. This gives the adjuster an opportunity to review the medical records and/or employment pay stubs. To schedule the telephone conference, call the adjuster a few days after the Demand Letter has been mailed and confirm the adjuster's receipt of the letter and records. Ask to set a date and time certain for the phone call. Ask if the adjuster will initiate the call, or shall you? In either case, make sure you are available on that date, at the proper time. Scheduling this phone call is important and will save you lots of mental and emotional duress in the negotiating process.

NEGOTIATING WITH THE CLAIMS ADJUSTER: It is becoming increasingly difficult for injured victims to negotiate a fair settlement with auto insurance claims adjusters, primarily because fewer lawyers are willing to advocate for whiplash victims. In the 1970s it was common for a garden variety whiplash case to settle for three times the amount of the medical bills. That is seldom the case today, the result of several decades of a strategy designed to discourage attorneys from representing whiplash victims. Forcing lawyers to try smaller personal injury whiplash cases has been highly effective. Auto insurance companies employing the strategy of *Delay, Deny and Defend* means plaintiff lawyers simply cannot afford to take a whiplash case that will require them to invest more time and effort for which they can expect to be paid. A lawyer is in business. A business with overhead: rent, employees, supplies and materials, professional dues, family obligations, etc. The product attorneys have to offer is their time and expertise. If an investment of time in your whiplash case will not yield a return sufficient to cover their expenses and justify their efforts, they will no longer take whiplash cases. This has happened over the past three decades. Auto insurance companies are willing to spend more to defend a whiplash case than it could have been settled for, to discourage lawyers from representing soft tissue cases. This is another reason why it is important to hire the right lawyer (see page 73) if you choose not to represent yourself.

Notwithstanding the above, it is still possible for a knowledgeable whiplash victim to negotiate a fair settlement if the case is evaluated from the view and perspective of the insurance company. To give yourself the best shot at a fair settlement, it is important you carefully monitor your telephone conversations with the adjuster. Just as with the doctor, do not overstate *or understate* your symptoms, or their effect on your activities of daily living. At the beginning of every phone conversation be sure to ask, *"Is this phone call being recorded?"* The reason for that question is obvious: anything you say may be used at a later date against you.

The adjuster will not be doing his/her job unless they inquire about your injuries. It is important, especially within the first six weeks of the incident, that you make no statements about the nature and extent of your injury. The reason: you simply will not know how serious your injuries are for at least six weeks. This author recommends you do not get into too much detail about your injuries for at least six months. The adjuster will press you for a status report with questions like:

"Are you feeling better?" "How would you rate your pain on a scale of 1 to 10?" "Are you able to do your normal day to day activities?"

Prior to negotiating with the adjuster, the safest response to these types of questions is:

"I am treating with Dr. _____. He/she has not released me from care at this time. I will contact you when I have been released."

"I am still having pain relating to the injuries caused by your insured's negligence. It varies from day to day, depending on my activities. I will contact you when I have been released."

Here are some key points to keep in mind as you prepare to discuss your case with the claims adjuster.

1. You must be willing to hire an attorney if you cannot reach a fair settlement within thirty to sixty days *after* you have reached maximum medical improvement and submitted the demand letter. The claims adjuster needs to know you are serious about hiring a lawyer if you cannot get the matter resolved by a date certain.

2. It is important to remember that insurance adjusters, and their supervisors, are human beings also. By and large, if the adjuster is treated with respect and consideration, you will go far in achieving the maximum settlement value of the case.

3. Claims adjusters will not settle the case without documentation. The desire to close a file will not overcome their preservation instincts. Every settlement the claims adjuster makes is subject to some sort of scrutiny at a higher level. This means you must document the injury and its impact upon you and your family.

4. Claims adjusters, and their supervisors, rarely are persuaded by claims of pain and suffering, loss of consortium, mental and emotional anguish, and other subjective complaints. To settle a case, a claims adjuster needs hard facts, well documented.

5. Most claims adjusters prefer to close files, but they will not do so at the risk of their jobs. Closing a file is the primary goal for the claims adjuster. Again, the adjuster must be able to justify the settlement amount to his/her supervisor. If the settlement figures are widely apart, and you hire an attorney and file a lawsuit, the adjuster simply refers the case to the defense attorney on staff for the insurance company.

6. Some insurance companies settle, and some do not. Nationally, and in geographic regions throughout the US, some companies are known for their willingness to settle cases, while other refuse even when liability is clear. If you are dealing with an insurance company that has had success in defending rear-end collision cases, it is a waste of time trying to negotiate. Your time is better invested in finding a good lawyer (see page 73).

7. The threat of a lawsuit will not intimidate an insurance company into settling with you. In cases of clear liability, where damages are perceived as minimal, and injury is to soft tissue, an insurance company is likely to spend more in the defense of the matter than the case could have settled for. If there is comparative fault on your part, the same is true. Auto insurance companies do not want to give the impression to any injured party, or any plaintiff's attorney, they are willing to settle rear-end collisions cases for more than a minimal amount.

8. **The Statute of Limitations:** It is critically important you know the statute of limitations for your incident. Plainly stated, the statute of limitations is that period of time, beginning with the date of the incident, in which you must either settle your case, or file a lawsuit, or your claim is forever barred! The statute of limitations is set by each state. One state may have a two-year statute, the adjacent state

a three-year statute and another adjoining state a four-year statute of limitations. As an example, if your incident occurred on May 1, 2020 in State X, and the statute of limitations in State X is two years, you must either settle your case, or file a lawsuit, by May 1, 2022. To find out the statute of limitations for personal injury in your state, check online, call the local BAR Association, inquire of a personal injury lawyer, or ask the claims adjuster. If the claims adjuster is providing the information, ask him/her to put it in writing. Whichever method you choose, know the statute of limitations for your case.

TIPS ON NEGOTIATING WITH THE CLAIMS ADJUSTER: Following are a number of tips to help in the negotiation process with the claims adjuster *once you have been released by the treating physician.* Some will be more effective than others. All have been used successfully by personal injury attorneys in whiplash cases. Each is worthy of consideration and adaptation to your circumstances.

1. Be prepared. Review your demand letter and the supporting documents - medical records and pay stubs.

2. Be confident. If you have followed the suggestions listed herein you are in a much better position than most cases the adjuster is used to seeing with injured victims representing themselves.

3. Be attentive and take notes. Listen as the claims adjuster presents the insurance company's position. **Ask how the adjuster arrived at the settlement figure offered.**

4. Ask probing questions. Following are questions which you can use in response to the claims adjuster's statement you are not badly injured or that the demand is way out of line.

   - *Is there something about this case which I have failed to consider which requires me to reduce my demand by such a large amount?*
   - *Do you question the reasonableness of my medical bills?*

- *Is the doctor's opinion regarding the permanency of injury being questioned?*
- *Do you agree this injury has resulted in pain and suffering for me?*
- *Shouldn't I be entitled to compensation for that pain and suffering?*
- *Do you really believe a jury would award a figure that low after hearing all the facts and evidence?*
- *What is your estimation of the cost of the defense of this case if it goes to trial?*
- *Is this a "net" offer? (Will I get to keep all the money?)*

5. Be responsive. Few things detract more from your ability to negotiate with a claims adjuster than your failure to promptly return phone calls or answer correspondence.

6. Be reasonable. Accept a reasonable offer. Avoid "nickel and dime" negotiations.

7. Be firm. When you have arrived at the value of the case, and the difference between your value and the offer is substantial, don't be afraid to walk away from negotiations. Often claims adjusters will shoot a low-ball offer just to see how you will respond. Maintain a positive attitude and suggest negotiations be continued on another day. Walking away from the bargaining table shows the parity between negotiating parties. Sometimes a week or two of silence will go a long way to resolving differences of opinion. Wait a reasonable length of time and try again. The exception to this technique is if you are dealing with an insurance company which is notorious for not settling whiplash cases. Then it becomes necessary to hire a lawyer and file a lawsuit.

8. File when ready. If you have reached the point in negotiations where you remain a long distance apart, give the claims adjuster the "drop dead" date. If negotiations are not completed by that date, hire a lawyer (see page 73).

9. When (not if) the adjuster makes a ridiculously low offer, don't respond in anger or frustration. Especially in MIST type cases, it is not uncommon for the adjuster to give an extremely low offer. A display of emotion rarely will change an adjuster's mind.

10. The offer is not ridiculous, but it is not enough. Respond to the adjuster with, "I cannot accept that amount. Do you have any room to move?" If he/she says "No", and the amount just won't work for you, hire an attorney (see page 73).

INSURANCE COMPANY TACTICS: There are several tactics employed by auto insurance claims adjusters in negotiating settlements. They are worth mentioning here, if for no other reason than to keep you from being surprised.

No Response. You have supplied the claims adjuster with all the pertinent medical information, lost wage documentation and other information necessary to settle the case. You have documented everything in the Demand Letter, with a request for a telephone conference in two weeks. You called to confirm receipt of the Demand Letter but were not able to speak with the claims adjuster, and the call has not been returned. You wait expectantly for an acceptance to your demand, or more likely, a counteroffer. Neither arrive. Why?

1. Your demand letter was either lost or misplaced.

2. The claims adjuster has been too busy to address your claim.

3. The claims adjuster is stalling in order to achieve a lower settlement.

4. The insurance company never had any intentions of settling this case for more than nuisance value.

In the first three instances a telephone call to the claims adjuster is the best approach. If the matter can be resolved within the next week to ten days, refrain from hiring a lawyer. If, however, you fail to see any sincerity with respect to negotiations, or if you are comfortable the insurance company never had any intentions of settling, hire an attorney (see page 73).

The Authority Game. Every claims adjuster has authority to settle the case within certain limits, depending on the type of incident. If your incident falls within their parameters of settlement, there is no reason to prevent them from making an offer. Typically, the offer will be lower than their maximum authority, meaning they can go up in the negotiations to settle the case. If they are convinced your case warrants a settlement exceeding their authority, they can request additional authority from their supervisor. If they are constantly seeking authority or state their supervisor will not authorize any more for your case, ask to speak to the supervisor.

The Low Ball Offer. What do you do when the value you put on the case of $20,000 is met with an offer of $1,200? First, go back through the facts you used to evaluate your case. If your evaluation of the case was correct, then look at the possible motive for the low-ball offer.

It may be the adjuster is trying to coerce you into a lower settlement by virtue of a low offer; or, it may be the adjuster is employed by one of those insurance companies that would rather litigate than settle. If it is the latter, hire an attorney. Try asking the adjuster if he/she has any room to move, or if they can get additional authority to settle this case. If the answer is yes, review the next offer. If it is no, hire an attorney.

The Adjuster asks: What Will You Accept? This and the Low-Ball Offer are the two most common tactics used by claims adjusters. The intent of the adjuster is to get you to lower your demand. Rarely, if ever, does this result in a settlement. A good response is you will accept what has been stated in the demand letter. Then ask, "What do you value this case at?"

Offer Withdrawn. A tactic sometimes seen is the withdrawal or reduction of the offer previously made. This is done to shock you into begging for a return of the original offer. When the value is there, and you have documented your case, don't fall for this feeble attempt to get you to take a lower value.

Offer Only Good for Today. This is similar to Offer Withdrawn in that the intent is to put pressure on you to settle for a lesser amount. Most adjusters will give you a reasonable time to decide without trying to pressure you. Unless the statute of limitations is breathing down your neck, take enough time to reflect on the offer before responding. If the adjuster persists in saying the offer will be withdrawn tomorrow, then one must wonder whether their negotiations were made in good faith. It may be time to hire an attorney.

Settlement and Taxes. You have reached a settlement figure with the auto insurance company. Congratulations. You have successfully settled your whiplash personal injury case. You will be asked to sign a Release. Once signed, you will not be able to sue either the negligent person, or the insurance company, for the injury received in the incident. In many instances, if you are married, the auto insurance company may require your spouse to sign the Release as well. This is done because they may also have a claim for damages, even though they were not in the vehicle at the time of the incident. Your injury may have affected your spouse, and the auto insurance company is closing the books on this incident, once and for all.

Do I have to pay taxes on the settlement amount? Personal injury settlements are generally not taxable as income. However, to be certain you will be well advised to consult with a professional tax preparer.

CONCLUSION

This overview was intended to give you sufficient information to understand how and why your injury occurred; the myths auto insurance adjusters use in their negotiations with injured victims; alternative medical treatment options available; how to hire the right attorney for your incident, if necessary; and, how to negotiate a settlement with the auto insurance company on your own. Hopefully, this information will be helpful in your efforts to recover and receive a fair settlement.

Best of luck in all your endeavors and may you be restored to the same healthful condition you were in prior to the "incident".

BIBLIOGRAPHY OF REFERENCES

1. **Croft AC, Freeman MD,** Correlating Crash Severity with Injury Risk, Injury Severity, and Long-Term Symptoms in Low Velocity Motor Vehicle Collisions, *Med Sci Monit*, 2005;11(10):316-21

2. **Eis V, Sferco R, Fay P.** A Detailed Analysis of the Characteristics of European Rear Impacts. Proceedings 19th International Technical Conference on the Enhanced Safety of Vehicles, Washington DC, NHTSA, DOT HS 809-825, 2005.

3. **Robbins MC,** Lack of Relationship Between Vehicle Damage and Occupant Injury. SAE Paper No. 970494. Society of Automotive Engineers, 1997.

4. **Sturzenegger M, DiStefano G, Radanow BP, and Schnidrig A,** Presenting Symptoms and Signs After Whiplash Injury: The Influence of Accident Mechanisms, *Neurology*, 44:688-93. 1994.

5. **Macnab I:** Acceleration Extension Injuries of the Cervical Spine. Rothman and Simeone, The Spine, 1982.

6. **Seletz E:** Whiplash Injuries: Neurophysiological Basis for Pain and Methods Used for Rehabilitation, *J.A.M.A.* 168(13):150-155; 1958.

7. **Nordhoff, Lawrence S., Jr:** Motor Vehicle Collision Injuries, Biomechanics, Diagnosis, and Management, Second Edition, 2005, page 484.

8. **Hohl M:** Soft Tissue Injuries of the Neck in Automobile Accidents: Factors Influencing Prognosis. *J Bone Joint Surg* 56A, (8):1675-1682, 1974.

9. **Foreman and Croft:** Whiplash Injuries: The Cervical Acceleration/ Deceleration Syndrome. William & Wilkins, 1988.

10. **Teasell & McCain:** Painful Cervical Trauma, Williams & Wilkins, 1992.

11. **Lord S:** Cervical Flexion-Extension/Whiplash Injuries. *Spine:* State of the Art Reviews, Hanky & Belfus, Sept. 1993.

12. **White AA and Panjabi MM:** Clinical Biomechanics of the Spine, J.B. Lippincott Company, 1990.

13. **Macnab I:** The Spine, Saunders, 1982.

14. **Webb CB:** Whiplash: Mechanisms and Patterns of Tissue Injury, *J Aust Chiro Assoc*, June 1985.

15. **Turek, Samuel:** Orthopaedics: Principles and Their Application, J.B. Lippincott Co., 1977.

16. **Havsy AF:** Whiplash Injuries of the Cervical Spine and Their Clinical Seaquelae, *Am J of Pain Mang.* Jan 1994.

17. **Bamsley L:** Cervical Flexion-Extension/Whiplash Injuries, *Spine*: State of the Art Reviews, Sept. 1993.

18. **Ziegler PN:** The Relationship Between Shoulder Belt Fit and Occupant Protection. In: Proceedings of the 26th Annual Conference of the Association for the Advancement of Automotive Medicine. Ontario, Canada: *AAAM*; 1982:267-278. and,

19. **Backaitis SH, DeLarm L, Robbins DH:** Occupant Kinematics in Motor Vehicle Crashes. SAE Paper No. 820247. Warrendale, PA: Society of Automotive Engineers: 1982.

20. **Foret-Bruno JY, Dauvilliers F, Tarriere C:** Influence of the Seat and Head Rest Stiffness on the Risk of Cervical Injuries in Rear Impacts. 13th ESV Conference, Paris, France, 1991.

21. **Ameis A:** Cervical Whiplash: Considerations in the Rehabilitation of Cervical Myofascial Injury. *Can Fam Phys*, 32:1871-76, Sept. 1986.

22. **Chipman ML:** Risk Factors and Automobile Collisions: Age, Sex and Circumstances, in Proceedings 24th Annual Conference, AAAM, p 298, 1980.

23. **Bonnuccelli U, Pavese N, Lucetti C, Renna MR, Gambaccini G, Bernardini S:** Late Whiplash Syndrome: A Clinical and Magnetic Resonance Imaging Study. *Funct Neurol.* 2001; 16(3):289-291.

24. **Jeffreys E, McSweeney T:** Disorders of the Cervical Spine. London, UK: Butterworth; 1980.

25. **Jonsson H, Cesarini K:** Findings and Outcomes in Whiplash-Type Neck Distortions. *Spine*, Vol. 19, No. 24, 2733-2743, 1994.

26. **Omer PA**; A Physician-Engineer's View of Low Velocity Rear End Collisions, SAE Technical Paper Series (1992).

27. **Yoganadan N**: Anatomic Study of the Morphology of Human Cervical Facet Joint. *Spine*. 2003;28(20):2317-23.

28. **Kellett J**: Acute Soft Tissue Injuries—A Review of the Literature. *Med Sci Sports Exerc*. 18(5):489-500; 1986.

29. **Hunt TK, Hopf H, Hussain Z**: Physiology of Wound Healing. *Adv Skin Wound Care*. 2000;13(Suppl 2):S6-S11.

30. **Squires B, Gargan MR, Bannister GC**: Soft Tissue Injuries of the Cervical Spine: 15-Year Follow-Up. *J Bone Joint Surg* [Br], 1996;78-B:955-957. and,

31. **Watkinson A, Gargan MR, Bannister GC**: Prognostic Factors in Soft Tissue Injuries of the Cervical Spine. *Injury*. 1991;22:307-309.

32. **Green J**: Common Head, Neck, and Back Injuries. Malabar, FL: Robert E. Krieger; 1988.

33. **Galasko CS, Murray PM, Pitcher M, Chambers S**: Neck Sprains After Road Traffic Accidents: A Modern Epidemic. *Injury* (24)(3); 155-157 (1993).

34. **Brisson RJ**: A Prospective Study of Acceleration-Extension Injuries Following Rear-End Motor Vehicle Collisions. *J Musculoskeletal Pain*. 8:97-113, 2000.

35. **Hincapie CA**: Whiplash Injury is More Than Neck Pain: A Population-Based Study of Pain Localization After Traffic Injury. *J Occup Environ Med*, 2010;52(4):434-40.

36. **Mendelson G**: Not "Cured by a Verdict". *Med J Aust* 1982; 2:132-134.

37. **Maimaris C, Barnes MR, Allen MJ**: Whiplash Injuries of the Neck, *Injury*, 19(5):393-96, 1988.

38. **Evans RW**: Some Observations on Whiplash Injuries, *The Neurology of Trauma*, Vol. 10, No. 4, Nov. 1992.

39. **Haboubi NH**: Short-Term Sequelae of Minor Head Injury, *Disabil Rehabil*, 2001;23(14):635-638.

40. **Carroll LJ, Ferrari R, Cassidy JD**: Reduced or Painful Jaw Movement After Collision Related Injuries: A Population-Based Study. *J Am Dent Assoc*. 2007;138(1):86-93.

41. **Severinsson Y**: Jaw Symptoms and Signs and the Connection to Cranial Cervical Symptoms and Post-Traumatic Stress During the First Year After a Whiplash Trauma. *Disabil Rhabil,* 2010.

42. **Smith MC**: Analysis of Reals-World Rear-End Crash Occupants with TMJ. Society of Automotive Engineers, 1999.

43. **Schnabel M, Vassiliou T, Schmidt T, Basler HD, Gotzen L, Junge A**: Results of Early Mobilization of Acute Whiplash Injuries. *Schmers.* 2002;16(1):15-21.

44. Quebec Task Force on Whiplash-Associated Disorders, Spine, Vol.20, No. 8S, April 15, 1995.

45. **Eccles RW**: Whiplash / Personal Injury Excellence, 1993.

46. **Insurance Research Council**: Auto Injury Insurance Claims: Countrywide Patterns in Treatment, Cost, and Compensation. 2008 Edition.

47. **Gonyea MA**: The role of the Doctor of Chiropractic in the Health Care System in Comparison with Doctors of Allopathic Medicine and Doctors of Osteopathic Medicine. Washington, DC: Center of Studies in Health Policy, FCER; 1993.

48. **Steigerwald DP**: Management of Whiplash Induced TMJ Injuries. *ACA J Chiro*, March 1995, 67-70.

49. **Yoganandan N, Pintar FA**: *Frontiers in Whiplash Trauma*, IOS Press, pp348-371, 2000.

50. **Jakobsson L, Norin H, Jernstrom C**: Analysis of Different Head and Neck Responses in Rear-End Car Collisions Using a New Humanlike Mathematical Model, IRCOBI Conference 1994.

51. **Teasell RW** and **McCain GA**: Clinical Spectrum and Management of Whiplash Injuries, in *Painful Cervical Trauma: Diagnosis and Rehabilitative Treatment of Neuromusculoskeletal Injuries.* Williams & Wilkins, 1992.

52. **Foret-Bruno JY, Tarriere C, Le Coz JY**: Risk of Cervical Lesions in Real-World and Simulated Collisions, in 34th Proceedings, *AAAM*, p373-89, Scottsdale, 1990.

53. **Bunketorp L**: A Descriptive Analysis of Disorders in Patients 17 Years Following Vehicle Accidents. *Eur Spine J.* 2002;11(3):227-34.

54. **Carroll LJ**: Course and Prognostic Factors for Neck Pain in Whiplash-Associated Disorders [WAD]: Results of the Bone and Joint Decade 2000—2010 Task Force on Neck Pain and Its Associated Disorders, *Spine*, 2008;33(4S):1S-219S.

55. **Rosenfeld M**: Active Intervention in Patients with Whiplash-Associated Disorders Improves Long-Term Prognosis: A Randomized Controlled Clinical Trial. *Spine*. 2003;29(22):2491-8.

APPENDIX

May 15, 2020

John Q. Adjuster
ABC Insurance Company
1234 Alake Road
Suite 1250
Anytown, NY 12045

> Re: Your Insured: Debbie Defendant
> Your Claim #: API76Q2Z
> Date of Loss: August 26, 2019

Dear Mr. Adjuster:

I write today for the purpose of submitting a claim for injury and loss as a result of the above referenced incident. My doctor (or health care provider) has stated I have reached a static and stable condition. My most current medical records are included. This letter will serve as my request for the settlement amount disclosed herein.

Liability: As you are aware, liability is clear in this case. The Anytown, NY police department issued a citation to your insured for failure to operate a motor vehicle in a prudent manner. I was stopped for a red light at the intersection of State and 12th Street when your insured ran into the rear of my vehicle. The police report notes that Ms. Defendant was talking on her cell phone and not paying attention at the moment of impact. Clearly there was no negligence on my part and your insured was the sole and proximate cause of the collision.

Damages: The damage to the rear of my vehicle was $2,476.73, which my insurance company has paid, less my $500.00 deductible. Please note that in addition to the repairs to the bumper and right taillight assembly, the frame of my car was bent from the force of the impact. A claim is being made for the $500.00 deductible.

My physical injuries are described in the medical records as a severe cervical strain. Immediately following the collision, I was dizzy and disoriented. I had an instant headache and had to be helped from the car by the police officer on site. I was transported by ambulance to General Hospital. Their records are enclosed. The emergency room treating physician was Dr. Johnson, who prescribed 24 physical therapy sessions. The records from the physical therapist are enclosed.

Dr. Johnson referred me to Dr. Quigley for ongoing treatment. Both Dr. Johnson's and Dr. Quigley's records are enclosed. Dr. Quigley notes that many of the outdoor activities I previously enjoyed will likely cause discomfort and pain. These include tennis, hiking and kayaking. His recommendation is I discontinue tennis and kayaking as these will aggravate my neck, and only hike periodically. Tennis and kayaking were the activities I enjoyed with my family.

Medical Expenses: I have previously sent you all medical bills incurred to date. Attached is an itemized list with total expenditures of $8,243.52. These are reasonable charges for the treatment to date. In addition, Dr. Quigley states in his records I will need periodic maintenance treatment of $1,200.00 per year, for at least another five years, just to cope with the pain.

Permanent Impairment: Both the physical therapist and Dr. Quigley note in their records that I will more likely than not have future episodes of pain and disability as a result of this wreck; and, that I am more likely to be injured in another event, even if the forces involved are not great. Dr. Quigley also noted I am a candidate for early onset of arthritis, even though I am only 39 years old, because of this wreck.

Loss of Wages: As you are aware, I am an accountant with the firm of Harley & Troxell. As a result of your insured's negligence I was forced to miss work a total of six days, and to take another six day of personal time without pay. My loss of pay for those twelve days is $2,724.00.

CLAIM: On the basis of clear liability, medical bills, permanency of the injury, loss of income and the pain and inconvenience caused by your insured's negligence, the sum of $55,000 is requested. Listed below is an itemization of actual bills paid as a result of this incident.

Property Damage:	$ 500.00
Medical Bills:	8,243.52
Future Medical Bills:	6,000.00
Loss of Wages:	2,724.00
	$17,467.52

Given the fact I have kept you informed of the developments of my care and treatment, including providing all medical expenses, this offer is made for a period of ten days. If I have not received your acceptance of this offer, I shall proceed with hiring an attorney to pursue my best interests. Thank you for your consideration.

Sincerely,

Injured Victim

www.ingramcontent.com/pod-product-compliance
Lightning Source LLC
Chambersburg PA
CBHW060552100426
42742CB00013B/2522